THE LIFESPAN MOVEMENT

THE LIFESPAN MOVEMENT

A progression to finding purpose, and happiness

By

Nayana Williams

*"This book is a memoir. The names, characters and events are a
depiction of my own genuine experiences; however, some names and
events have been altered."*

ISBN: 978-976-96827 -0-2

Table of Contents

Dedication

To Devon, you mean the world to me.
To Elizabeth, my greatest inspiration.
To my loving son Milan, a star in the making.
To my dearest parents, Barbara and Daniel.
To everyone who has embarked on this journey with me, gratitude is the key to happiness... I dedicate this book to you all

Acknowledgements

Thank you to Devon, my life and business partner who joined me in giving birth to Lifespan. Thank you to David who worked ceaselessly to carry out the production agenda – you did great. Thank you to my sister, Bingy who has lent her support and creativity time and time again. Thank you to my parents – because of you I have a story to tell. Thank you to Dorrette and Miss Cynthia for their unwavering support which has allowed me to spread my wings. Thank you to Rodney, Melissa and Jessica for encouraging me to share a part of my story. Thank you to Sandra for mentoring the business to become a corporate entity with an effective Board. Thank you to the Chairwomen, the Directors and Cristina who have lent their expertise in governing the company over the years. Thank you to Team Lifespan for their dedication and hard work. Thank you to those unnamed persons who have supported me throughout my journey. Thank you to the book editing team who labored to make this book a reality. And thank you to the readers who will become inspired to create their own story...

Introduction

It was during one of the most challenging times in my life that I told myself that things had to be different, that there was more for me than what was being offered at that time; in that moment, I found myself believing that there was more in me to give. Since then, all the steps, failures, decisions, and choices that I have experienced propelled me towards my many outcomes. It kindled a flame, a deep desire that led me to harness every fiber of my being, strength and absolutely everything I could pull on from inside and channel it towards evolving, to becoming the version of me that would pave the way for what I was about to build— "My legacy".

This led me to building a business from scratch and scaling it in an industry dominated by men which took extra grit and tenacity. Nonetheless, I doubled down to create an iconic brand which is known throughout Jamaica, the Caribbean and other places outside this geographic region. It was through this that my purpose was unveiled, a new level of happiness immerged, and my financial freedom was unlocked. Through persistence and my inability to accept defeat, I was able to overcome the numerous trials that were thrown at me. I, a woman, found peace succeeding in my many roles. Some would say I have my hands full with it all – the role of a wife, mother, daughter, sister, successful entrepreneur, C.E.O and feminist.

I remember as a teenager I used to daydream about falling in love and getting married at twenty-two and having my first child at twenty-six. My vision became my reality to some extent when I got married at twenty-two but I had my first child at twenty-one years old. Also, when I was starting my business, we had to work with Plan B until we could go back to Plan A. My point is that a plan is put in place as a guide, but it can change along the way, as there are always unforeseen detours that you cannot plan for. The detours are the real lessons, and they're what makes life interesting. This is where growth and potential can come to fruition.

So many agendas come into play within the parameters of human interaction; there is greed, ambition, and self-enrichment at all costs, which get in the way of the vision. If I did not have my head firmly planted on my shoulders, there would have been a train wreck with various tracks going in numerous directions without the necessary stop and go signs to manage traffic flow. Sometimes the traumas of our past get in the way of realizing happiness. Therefore, I decided that I would not become a product of my bad experiences but rather of both the good and bad. I look at each experience as learning something new. There is always a takeaway that can be applicable to a future experience.

While I am motivated by ensuring financial security for me and my family, I am also motivated by building up my community and alleviating poverty. I recognize that there must be steady growth, otherwise there will be continuous decline. The same principles of life apply to business. There are some of us who are only motivated by money, and this is what creates the discord; there is no connection to the possibilities that exist outside of what is known. These are the same people who do not believe in team and community empowerment. They are all for self-enrichment only. Therefore, I find myself being constantly attacked from all sides while I continue to work on and strategize building up the company. There are times when I have felt beaten and bruised, but I get up the very next morning and I go on, because I have no other choice. Just as I gave birth to my children, I gave birth to this company.

I have communicated a vision and put it into action. Everyone that is a part of the business has contributed to making it what it is today. Sitting in the driver's seat means I am the person steering the vehicle. It is my duty to navigate in the right direction, which is a massive responsibility. I need to always have the right information at my fingertips, and most importantly, I have to be decisive.

Throughout my journey, I have felt like a vessel inspired by a force greater than myself. Bringing this legacy of Lifespan has positively affected the lives of so many others, including my family members, employees, consumers, customers, suppliers, and other stakeholders.

This book captures the essence and the journey of the Lifespan movement. The business was birthed from a determination to cancel out heartbreak and create purpose and financial security. It was an opportunity to assist others by creating employment for people within the community. Starting Lifespan was also an opportunity to define a different type of corporate culture, one in which the environment became harmonious and happy without neglecting hard work and determination.

The start-up stage was the most difficult, since I was a brand-new female business leader. Yet I also found that the larger Lifespan became, the larger the obstacles that followed. Each obstacle continues to challenge me to reach for the next level, both personally and professionally.

Different stages of progression are inevitable on the quest to become an innovative leader. When change occurs, growth occurs simultaneously. Life is a series of changes and challenges, which work hand-in-hand together.

Part of progression is understanding your environment and what you personally need to succeed. When I felt like I needed more recreational space, I would set out to create this. Nature is my soul's calling, and I know I can sit and think through any difficult question or situation when I'm outside, staring at the sea.

There have been many times when I felt built-up pressure of others' expectations, where I needed to fully grasp the numerous dimensions of each relationship I had in my life. As an entrepreneur, you'll find that some of your loved ones' values and morals do not align with your own. Treasure your own belief system, as that's what makes you a strong, powerful leader. Before I understood this lesson, I remained a "peacekeeper" in many instances, and I would suffer the consequences most of all. I felt isolated when this occurred, and it became more difficult to maintain my composure, make decisions, lead a business, and satisfy all of my personal responsibilities.

Every year I undergo a different phase, both professionally and personally. Life is a continuous process of growth. We must undergo continuous transformation through various experiences. If we settle with stagnation, we are stuck in place, forever wondering, "What if I had made a different choice?" My hobbies continue to be an indication and an integral part of my personal growth. One year, I began music lessons to learn how to play the violin; when I realized I was just creating noise pollution in my home, I moved on to oil painting. Though I wasn't necessarily the best in the class, I didn't care. I only cared about learning a new skill set. There's always something new to learn in life, and this is how I live my life. I continue to embrace the aging process as well, understanding that while I become older, it doesn't mean I can't learn.

While I remain physically present at Lifespan as much as possible, I have come to acknowledge that I'm much more productive and efficient with my work in the early hours of the morning at my home office. As an entrepreneur, we must strive to understand how we meet our goals and deadlines, and part of this work is keeping track of our productivity.

My past experiences have taught me that I must pursue new ones, no matter how hard they seem. Sometimes, life gets in the way, and it's a matter of settling for a compromise. It's important to differentiate between what a compromise means to you, and what a compromise means to those around you. Settling can be at the expense of something near and dear to us. I've slowly come to realize that what I perceive to be true within my morals and values may not be perceived the same way by others in my life. In order to continue to allow yourself to change and grow, you must also respect the fact that everyone sees and thinks differently. Gratitude continues to be a rooted value in my life, and I'm grateful for every single person I've met, because my past experiences have allowed me to become the woman I am today.

One of the greatest lessons I've taken away from all of my experiences is that we are all alike yet different; I cannot expect others to think that my way is the only way. Throughout the grueling process of starting Lifespan and continuing the movement, I've also realized that though I may be related to others by blood, this does not mean that we hold the same morals, values, and think the same way. We are not extensions of one another; instead, we have our own thoughts and continue to have different opinions. It's what makes ideas become realities, the fact that every single individual has a different perspective. The two mantras I live by are:

For every action, there is a reaction. Do good, and good will follow you.

For me, I measure my success by my happiness. Once I enjoy what I am doing and achieve the required results, I am happy. Life is a state of progression for me. When I recognize that my team, my family, and I are all happy and thriving, that's the ultimate way to know how successful I've become.

An idea for a business alone cannot withstand the test of time.

You must do your research, identify the consumer need you are filling, formulate an action plan, gather your resources, and then begin. There are no magic bullets in business. Having a great work ethic, passion, purpose, and resilience are imperative qualities for a business leader to manifest. Again, gratitude plays a large role in the success of business. Treat others with courtesy and respect. Constantly evaluate the business as well as yourself and pursue growth at every level. Be willing to step out of your comfort zone. Be willing to challenge yourself. If you are not willing to face discomfort and obstacles which cannot be side-stepped, then you are not willing to face life for what it is. To succeed in your career requires the same principles and more in succeeding as an entrepreneur. It is about never giving up. It is about having no other choice but to continue. It is about changing the status quo. It is about being courageous. It is about defying all the odds against you. It is about standing strong in your personal values. It is about rewarding yourself at the end of the day. But it is mostly about focusing on the positives all the way and seeing that vision, setting those goals to reach that vision, and being proactive in reaching those goals.

When you've identified the business you want to pursue, you then need to evaluate your "why" statement. Why do you want to pursue this particular business? How will it affect your life? The economy? Your community? Understanding your "why" connects you to your true purpose.

The next step is to formulate the goals of your business. What are your business targets? What are the necessary action steps needed in order to achieve these targets? What resources are required, and how can you acquire them? How can you formalize your business with the relevant statutory organizations?

Once all of these questions have been answered, it's time to define your Plan A and Plan B; you'll want to have fallback plans in case Plan A doesn't pan out. This roadmap will ultimately help you before you embark on your entrepreneurial journey. Most people fail to realize that what they can see physically happening in front of them is only 25% of the entire business, and the other 75% is unseen.

Making the decision to become an entrepreneur is not an easy one; it is a complete mindset makeover. You allow your mind to conceive a vision and take the necessary actions for it to become a reality. Some people decide to keep their jobs while pursuing entrepreneurship. While this may be the logical thing to do for some, becoming successful at entrepreneurship requires your undivided attention. It requires the willingness to make sacrifices. You have to be willing to give up your comforts and take on a world of uncertainty, knowing you are a hundred percent certain about what you are doing. Be willing to survive on the basic necessities while you feed the business with your time and energy. You have to program your mind for success, and even when all seems lost at times, you have to get up, brush yourself off, and start again.

Having one foot inside of your vision won't make your vision a reality. Your whole body must dive head-first into the business. Make sure your mind, body, and soul are completely up to the task as one entity. You may become scared, frustrated, angry, confused, or a myriad of other emotions at times. Programme your mind to be fearless, and plunge into your business vision without room for any other alternatives. This is your only choice.

While you may sacrifice nice clothes, fancy meals, or a variety of other luxuries, make sure you never sacrifice your health, family, morals, or your sanity. If you find that any of these aspects of your life are not up to par, ask yourself how you can change your day-to-day tasks. See where you're spending your time and energy, and understand that while you have the vision, delegation is also necessary to see success in business. Investing your time and effort into something that won't bring you any returns isn't worth your time. Consider what self-improvement means to you, and how you can continuously improve yourself. Once you feel driven to fully see your ultimate business vision, it's time to pursue your dreams. Becoming an entrepreneur isn't for the faint of heart, and it isn't for everyone. But you'll know if this is your cup of tea.

Part 1:
The Early Years

Chapter 1

Granny

I woke up on the left side of the bed. As I slowly blinked my eyes open, I immediately saw my grandmother's straight, shoulder-length black hair beside me. My older brother lay sleeping – probably dreaming – on her right. My dolls, which I was only allowed to play with once per day, stared at me with jet-black eyes from the top of the closet.

"Granny?" I gently nudged her, excited to go to the farm with her.

"Oh, good morning, mi grand chile," she said sleepily, rising up in her pink nightie.

As I laid in bed while she got dressed, I couldn't wait for the aroma of hot chocolate boiled in fresh cow's milk to fill the three-bedroom board house.

Twenty minutes later, my brother, Nicky, groggily woke up, and we both walked barefoot on the red, polished hardwood floors towards the delightful smell emanating from the detached kitchen.

"Breakfast is ready!" Granny called out.

My brother and I walked over to the small verandah, watching the waves form in the sea just a few kilometers away. Just a year later, I would be swimming in those waves daily with my siblings, drinking coconut water and eating guavas.

As we sipped our hot chocolate sprinkled with cinnamon and nutmeg, we took bites of the roasted salt fish mixed with red pepper and garlic in coconut oil which was served with roasted breadfruit – my own little five-year-old heaven.

Granny finally settled into a chair and told us another one of her stories.

"As you know, chile, Maihi and Happa came to Jamaica in 1916 from a small rural village in India," she explained. "My mother was originally from Delhi and my father was from a humble background in Madras, one of the untouchables, a low born, son of the caste system which existed in India. My mother ran away from her well-to-do home from a high-born family to be with my father who was the love of her life. My father, looking for a better life and wanting to raise a family, took my mother and boarded a ship to Jamaica. The passage to Jamaica was paid for by becoming indentured servants on the Grays Inn plantation in Annotto Bay, St. Mary which was owned by Charlie Pringle, a colonial who was originally from England. After seven years as indentured servants living on the plantation, they started getting paid two shillings per week, so Happa started saving and he purchased his first ten-acre block of land in Belfield, St. Mary for two pounds ten shillings and planted his own farm. He continued to save and gradually bought the adjoining lots and eventually accumulated fifty-eight acres of land. He farmed banana, cocoa, coffee, breadfruit, and other crops. He would sell the bananas to a co-op for export to England. The other crops were sold on the local market. They also raised cows and goats and sold meat on the local market."

I listened to my grandmother intently as she told her story. My great grandfather, Happa, died at the age of one hundred and two years old, one week before I was born, while my great grandmother had died several years before. I was dazzled and in awe of my great grandparents, who barely had anything but decided to create a new life for themselves in a brand-new country. Their story inspired me throughout the years to one day build my own business, take chances, and believe in myself, just as they believed in a better future for themselves and their family.

Before we left for the farm, I put on a beautiful, flowery, cotton dress. At five years old, my favorite color was blue – I never liked red, and Granny knew that. All of my dresses were exquisite, and handmade by Granny.

On the hour-long walk, I told Granny, Big Papa, and my brother all about who I wanted to be when I grew up.

"Maybe I'll be a doctor so I can make everyone get better!" I exclaimed.

"Sandy, last week you wanted to be a diplomat," Granny reminded me. "And the week before that you said you wanted to be a lawyer!"

I giggled, remembering those conversations. Then everyone laughed with me. I really intended to be and pursue as many professions as I could.

"Sandy, you can be anything you want to be when you grow up," Granny told me. "You don't have to decide now. You're only a child! Just don't depend on your husband," she whispered, and we laughed some more.

*

As we approached the farm, I happily scrambled down from Big Papa's shoulder and smelled the fresh, warm dirt. April is usually the last hot, dry month before the rainy season begins in Jamaica. Temperatures can range between 75 degrees Fahrenheit and 85 degrees Fahrenheit. The following month of May is usually the crab season as the crab holes get filled with water from the excessive rain. The crabs are hunted at night by the locals, and they are usually boiled or curried down in coconut milk and served with boiled bananas. I would not be taken to the farm in May, as it would be too wet, and the farm would not be as frequented by the elders.

The grass needed to be cut, and since I was too short to walk through it myself, Big Papa and my brother usually took turns carrying me. We cut across the sugarcane fields and found the banana and plantain walk. Sampling ripened bananas at the farm was one of my favorite pastimes, while my brother loved to peel the fresh sugar cane using his teeth and I would patiently wait for him to give me a piece to chew on as the sweet and sticky juice dripped all over my hands.

When we arrived home from the farm, Big Papa would make us special protein shakes using eggs, orange juice and aloe juice, which was his favorite, then we would all sit together and drink. My grandfather was a quiet, unassuming, and hardworking man. On Sunday mornings after returning from his fishing trips, he would sit and mend his fish pots and fishing nets. He would demonstrate how to use the wooden fishing net needle and I would sit and watch, fascinated. Sometimes I would walk with my granny to the seaside to meet the boat and Big Papa would take me for a short boat ride which would be the highlight of my entire day. As I grew older, I would go fishing with him, especially throughout high school. On Sunday afternoons, he bought everyone ice cream from the Krazy Jim ice cream truck and occasionally told us stories about his parents.

I didn't know it then, but it would be the last time the four of us would be together at the farm. Several months later, my life would change drastically. My favorite person in the world – Granny – would pass away after surgery for cervical cancer, and my brother and I would move into my parents' house with our younger siblings.

This was my first experience dealing with grief. I was only six years old by then, but I understood that my Granny was never coming back in the flesh. The bond I had with her couldn't be recreated with anyone else in my family, despite my affection for my parents. The reality of Granny leaving me here alone impacted me greatly, as I always felt loved, protected, and cherished by her.

My mother, who was pregnant with her sixth child at the time, had her hands full with my younger siblings, and I was expected to help around the house. My toys were strewn about for everyone's enjoyment. The routine I had set in stone with Granny and my brother was thrown out the window as quickly as a 100-metre dash sprinter.

The bed I once shared with Granny and my brother was no more. Instead, I was forced to sleep with all of my siblings in a single bedroom with just two double beds. My three brothers shared a bed sporting a soccer quilt that Granny had made years ago, and my sister and I slept underneath pink floral sheets. My baby sister had the fortune of sleeping in my parents' bedroom.

The once quiet mornings I treasured became full of screaming matches, tantrums, and hair-pulling. In order to feel centered once again, I took refuge underneath the bed, where the pink sheets barely touched the blue rug covering a part of the spotless, terrazzo tiles. Books took up the majority of space under there, and I relished in the ability to take myself out of the present and into a brand-new world. And there were so many worlds to choose from. While my mother was cooking, cleaning, and tackling the piles of laundry, I chose to stay far away from the noise and let myself pretend I was a princess, or an emperor, or just a girl with big goals and dreams. Possibilities were endless when I picked up a book. By the time I was twelve years old, I had read the Bobbsey

Twins, Nancy Drew, and the Hardy Boys series. As a teenager, I read every romance novel I could get my hands on. I needed to know that romance existed. The older I became, the more I read. My favorite authors included James Patterson, Sidney Sheldon, Sandra Brown, Nora Roberts, V.C. Andrews, and so many more. One character in *Bloodline* by Sidney Sheldon specifically resonated with me – Elizabeth Williams. I could see myself within her. Elizabeth would become my unseen mentor throughout my life. Whenever I had a dilemma, I would consider what Elizabeth would do in my exact situation. While she wasn't perfect, she exhibited power and strength, which profoundly influenced my life. Due to my constant reading, I had also understood another fact about myself: I was a descendant of slaves and indentured servants brought to Jamaica from Africa and India. I considered myself lucky and fortunate to be where I was; I lived in a peaceful home by the sea and was loved by many family members, and I didn't take these blessings in my life for granted.

Every morning, I frowned as I saw my mother working so hard to keep our house tidy, only to find cow's milk and guava jam spread across the rug in mere seconds. It's difficult to keep a clean house with six children under the age of seven, a feat my mother seemed to have mastered. I knew that when I grew up, I did not want to have to do all these domestic chores, as my mother seemed miserable. The combination of observing my mother's emotions and deepening my knowledge of the world through books allowed me to see a bright future of limitless possibilities for myself. I was a dreamer and I had visions of conquering life and becoming everything I wanted to be, from a rock star to the leader of a business empire.

Chapter 2

A Cloudy Evening

At that time in my life, I turned six years old, I was told that I was like a bright shining star; I paraded around the house with the most beautiful smile, always jubilant, extremely inquisitive, and talkative. But in just one evening, my entire personality changed. It's incredible to think that now, as an adult, I experienced so much love and happiness, yet the action of someone else's wrongdoing took my childhood innocence away from me.

I overheard my mother talking to another family member about our dog, Big Head. He ran into the street and was hit by a car and died. No one mentioned this to me directly, and as I listened, I felt hot tears sprinkle down my already burning cheeks. I had a fever which had risen significantly that evening, and I had been drifting in and out of sleep for hours at that point, cozying up in my parents' bed. It was only a few weeks earlier that my granny had passed as well.

During that fuzzy night, I opened my eyes and saw one of my adult male cousins standing over me. I had never been particularly close with him. I was just aware that he visited my grandfather regularly. He lived some distance away in another parish and was staying longer than usual with other relatives who were also visiting. He was quite rotund and had beady eyes and an oversized stomach. At the time, I wasn't quite sure it was even him, since I was still dizzy with a high fever. I had never spent any alone time with him, so I was immediately confused as to why he would be standing over me, especially in my parents' bedroom.

I attempted to call out, "Mummy!" yet when I tried, my throat became drier; I felt thirsty and weak. I had fallen back asleep, and when I awoke, I was being carried by this same cousin from the bathroom and into my parents' room once again. I could hear my mother's voice from the verandah, and I tried to call out to her, but I was too weak.

"Shhh," he whispered to me. "This'll be our little secret."

I could barely understand what he was saying or what he meant; his presence just felt unnatural and disturbing. I became frightened as I started to be aware of my surroundings. My head throbbed, I could feel the heat of the fever on my skin, yet I was cold and shivering and there was a slight burning sensation between my thighs as if my skin was rubbed raw. The next thing I remember was my mother sponging me down as though I were an infant again and I fell asleep. I woke up the next morning with flashbacks of the night before haunting me, and I became both fearful and sad that my dog had died, my grandma had died, and that I felt like I was no longer sure who I could trust in my own home, besides my older brother. But he was away, meeting his biological mother; we were half-siblings, yet he was my ultimate protector in childhood.

The magnitude of this loss of innocence set in, and in order to cope with my loss, I buried this memory deep inside of myself for years and years. Though I did try to tell a couple of relatives, the words just wouldn't come out in a way that made sense, as I did not really understand what had happened.

At six years old, you do not think about the possibility of a known relative hurting you. You are entirely focused on your childish endeavors, feeling safe without a care in the world. At least, that's how I was before this horrendous night. There was a feeling of loneliness, as though I could never fully trust anyone ever again, which ultimately led me to become quieter and more reserved in any social setting. My parents had made sure that I was a strong girl from a young age, teaching me to love and respect myself. I felt my self-esteem completely dissipate within one night. Many years later, I realized that the secret was that my adult cousin had molested me and the feeling I felt for so long was that of being violated. Luckily, he had never tried again, maybe because I made sure I was never alone in his presence. I hid myself from the world by becoming extremely reserved and shy. I felt like there was something wrong with me. My parents had taught my siblings and I to always be kind to others, especially older relatives. Yet I couldn't bring myself to be kind to someone who had breached my innocence and changed the way I viewed the world. I soon developed a hatred towards him, and whenever I would see him at a family function, I would immediately go the other direction to avoid being in his presence even for a moment. When I became a teenager, I never saw this cousin again and I later learned he had died of an obesity-related disease. I felt a sense of relief that I would never have to encounter him again; it also allowed me to release the hatred I felt towards him.

Growing up, I stayed away from boys until I met my husband. There were various reasons for this, one of those reasons was what happened to me that particular night. Yet I was only able to come to this realization years later. After I had my first child, I became aware that I was overly protective of her to the point where I was uncomfortable leaving her in the presence of any male besides her father. I came to understand that a part of my life, and my personality, was partially stolen away from me. As I gradually began to understand what had happened to me, another incident occurred when I was a teenager – a female cousin's husband fondled my breasts when I sat in a car next to him, while his wife was driving the car. I boxed his hand away, but I told no one. Devastation and shock flooded my mind during and after this incident, and I avoided him like the plague. As an adult, I realized I did not want to hold onto these negative emotions any longer. Being a victim of one, or in my case, two, sexual assaults was dreadful enough, but I chose to let go and forgive the wrong that was done to me. I have not forgotten what these people did to me, but in order to move my life forward in a positive direction, I needed to be able to look back on these experiences and accept that they happened to me, while also acknowledging that I was not at fault. I was a child, and then a teenager. I did not deserve what happened to me. According to rainn.org, more than two out of every three sexual assaults go unreported. I was a part of that statistic. I also understand that these experiences are important to acknowledge, and I'm no longer burdened with these secrets of my past.

Chapter 3

A Report Card

I came home from school with an excellent report card at eight years old. In those early years, teachers scored students based on their level of participation, reading level, and overall academic performance. I walked home and slowly tiptoed through the open doorway, hoping to avoid running into my aunt. I had become even closer to my parents in the past two years; however, my father was out working during the days, and my mother couldn't keep up with household chores alone. So, my Aunt Ruthcid came to live with us, and I always had a deep longing to leave the room when I encountered her. Aunt Ruthcid was a victim of her own limiting beliefs, and she wore this proudly, like it was an achievement of sorts. My siblings and I detested her constant criticism, which on this day was as brutal as always. She was in the kitchen as usual, mopping the floor. I tried to tiptoe slowly through the living room to avoid her, asking God to protect me just this one day. I could see the clean purple sheets draped across the bed in my bedroom, but my relief only lasted for a millisecond as I heard, "Sandy, I see you. Stop avoiding me, I just cleaned the floor. Come here."

I held back tears as I longingly left the vision, I held of reading by myself underneath my purple sheets. All I wanted was to sneak into my room and be left alone to read. I didn't think much about receiving an excellent report card. I felt that school was just a requirement of life and earning a good grade was something I needed to do in order to propel myself forward; I really did not get excited about it as it was the norm for me then to get excellent grades. My mother and father would be the ones to get excited and I looked forward to showing my report to them as I liked to see them happy. They told me that in order to get a good job later in life, I needed to excel in school. Aunt Ruthcid couldn't care less, all she was concerned with was keeping the house clean and being admired by male suitors who would call on her at times.

"What's that you have in your hand?" She snatched my report card, looking it over with her dark, forlorn eyes. Her expression shifted suddenly, and she started berating me about how lazy I was.

"You think just because you get this report card, you're suddenly excused from doing anything?" She was speaking fast in her usual loud tone.

I stood frozen in the middle of the living room, looking at her frightfully. The bright incandescent lights, the floor with the black specks shining back at me, and the dark brown yet scratched wooden table were all blurry as a single tear fell down my face.

My brother overheard the one-sided conversation and joined us. Besides my Daddy, my older brother, Nicky, had always tried his best to protect me.

"What do you want in here, Nicky?" Aunt Ruthcid always referred to my older brother nicely as she seemed to prefer boys over girls.

"Just want to show Sandy a new drawing I did,' he said, as he tried to divert her attention away from me.

Ruthcid laughed and pointed her finger toward me.

"Who do you think you are, parading in here like that after I just mopped the floor?" She recoiled, crushing up my report card. She glared at me. "You don't need this. It's just a piece of paper. It doesn't mean that you're smart or anything, so stop trying to be better."

My brother gently took my hand in his, and we walked quickly toward the verandah. Tears started to flood my eyes. Aunt Ruthcid was the only person who had ever made me cry.

"Don't let her get to you, Sandy. She just likes to find faults with everything. We just have to deal with her. Next time, hide your report card in your bag so she can't see it."

"I…was…just…so…well…I…wanted…to…show…Mummy…" I was hyperventilating in between words.

"I know, Sandy, I know. Listen, Barbara appreciates Ruthcid's help very much, and she needs the help so don't pay much attention to her. We have to ignore her. Can you do that?" My older brother was my mother's stepson and he always referred to my mother by her first name, Barbara.

I nodded. I looked up to my brother, so I trusted his judgement. I already felt better after being reassured by him.

"Okay, good." He smiled, showcasing his straight white teeth with his eyes crinkling at the edges. "Now wipe your eyes and let me show you how to draw a cartoon!"

Chapter 4

I'll Race You to the River

I stared out at the endless expanse of blue to the horizons where the sky met the sea. This was the view from my verandah. It was still early and the plan for the day was to cook out at the riverside. I sat on the verandah and waited for my older cousins, Joy and Patsy. Growing up, my community was extremely close-knit. My cousins lived a short walk away, and other neighbourhood children would frequent our yard and join us for swimming sessions in the sea on the weekends and during the summer holidays.

I soon saw Joy walking up with her older sister, Patsy, along with my younger cousins trailing behind them. They were both wearing their signature black one-pieces with long flowing skirts, and their medium length, black hair had been braided the day prior. I had outgrown my swimsuit and my parents had not bought me a new one, so I was wearing shorts and tank tops; I actually preferred this as I was already very conscious of how revealing swimsuits were, or how wearing one was viewed by our small churchgoing community. I did have a couple of friends who wore their two-piece suits never caring about what anyone had to say. Even with all the criticism and sly remarks from the ladies in the neighbourhood, which continued for as long as I could remember, never deterred my friends or my older cousins who were considered rebels for being comfortable with their bodies and in what they wanted to wear. I always admired their ability to speak their minds clearly and thoughtfully.

"Sandy, let's go!" Gia exclaimed.

"Hold on, don't we have to wait for the younger ones?"

"No mon, they'll catch up! I'll race you there!"

I didn't want to lose the race, yet I knew I needed to wait for our younger cousins and my siblings. Luckily, I spotted them and yelled out, "We're racing to the river! Catch us!"

My older cousins – who were in their early thirties at the time – supervised us. They always brought the biggest beach towels, snacks, and sand toys for our adventures together. We walked for two miles to where the river flowed into the sea. Though I swam in the sea every single day each summer, walking to the river with my cousins was a bright yet rare opportunity to spend quality time with them, basking in our island of Jamaica's gorgeous rays of sun. During these excursions we would eat guavas and drink coconut water by the sea; we picked sea grapes and pounded almonds that littered the shores during our walk. By the time we reached the river mouth, we were hot and ready to go swimming.

"Tag, you're it!" Gia called out, and the band of children, including myself, ran along the riverside, splashing and wadding. Gia was Patsy's eldest daughter who was the same age as me.

While we gallivanted, my older cousins would do the cooking – roasting breadfruit and yam while we played. The freedom of being one with the water never left me – I still enjoy swimming to this day.

"Oh! I caught a janga!" Bingy cried out, dangling a small, black-eyed shrimp by its tail. "And here's another one! Sandy, here, take one!"

I grabbed a handful of squirming, slippery jangas, bringing them outside their comfort zone and into the world of the sand and sun, where they would soon be roasted for all of us to enjoy.

After laughing, playing, and feasting all day with family, we took our time walking the two miles back, stopping along the way to splash in the sea and pick more grapes. When we got home, my older cousins said we had some time to play in the backyard, and even though we were exhausted, we didn't want the day to end. The ten of us, my siblings, cousins, and I, danced in the yard to our favorite music – a variety of reggae, dancehall, pop, and country. It didn't really matter to me what was on the radio – I just loved to dance, especially with my family. We always had the best time enjoying the whole day outside with family.

The coconut trees greeted us fondly, as did the natural wood benches constructed by my little sister just a year prior. Abandoned train tracks stood to the south of the yard separated by a barbed wire fence and a pig pen, where our pet pig Reeni lived. My pet goat, Betty, had a pen adjacent to Reeni's. Though goat meat was popular in Jamaica when I was growing up, I neglected to have any.

"Sandy, please put Reeni back in her pen."

I knitted my brows in a frown, as I frequently did at ten years old, but obliged. I never dared say "no" to my mother; I had witnessed my younger siblings doing that and she would tell them to never answer her back and give them a spanking. As the eldest daughter, I was treated well by my parents growing up; I was never spanked, and they always commended my disciplined behavior. I never wanted to disappoint my parents.

Throughout the dance party, we took breaks to drink coconut water and ate June plum and guavas. I always thought it was amazing how I ate so much during those summers, yet I remained stick thin. It was probably from all of the dancing, swimming, and laughing. After all, laughing for ten to fifteen minutes burns between ten and forty calories, according to Vanderbilt University.

Soon after, our parents called us into the house for dinner time. My cousins dispersed and went to their homes while my siblings and I went to our house for dinner. Even though we would see our cousins bright and early the very next morning, we already missed them.

An array of fried fish, rice 'n peas, and cabbage salad decorated our plates on our large, wooden mahogany dining room table. We didn't even bother changing out of our swim clothes – we just sat down, still ravenous from being outside all day. A good meal always made me feel happy and fulfilled. I'd like to think the family dinners we had growing up influenced my decision to have family meals when I later became a mother.

I headed to my room after, feeling stuffed and anxious to bathe and read my Nancy Drew book before lights out. We were fortunate enough that my parents were able to add more rooms to our house, so I was able to have my very own room for the first time in my whole life. I fell asleep that night dreaming of the sea and the river, and echoes of endless laughter put a smile on my face in the early hours of the morning when I awoke for church the next day.

Chapter 5

Wear Your Sunday Best

My weekends were consumed with religion until I was six years old. I attended a Baptist church on Sundays with Granny and went to a Seventh Day Adventist church on Saturdays with my mother.

Granny would wear her Sunday best, as would all the ladies in the neighbourhood. I was expected to wear my white or purple flowered dress each week, along with a ribbon tied at the end of my single braid which fell almost to my waist. Very few memories stick with me to this day, yet I do remember one important thing: Granny never left for church without her Bible and her leather purse. Granny was fiercely independent and a no-nonsense, practical woman. She made her own dresses, and her handbag was handmade with leather from cowhide which was left to cure in the sun for many days. Her shoes were purchased from the local 'Batta" store in Annotto Bay. I especially liked her purse as it was crafty looking and fitted so much with her personality. When I asked her why she did not have a colored handbag like all the other ladies, she explained that her bag was stronger, and water could not soak through if it rained. This made a lot of sense in my young mind, though I also liked the purses in various colors that the other ladies carried. Mummy did not allow me to go to that church after Granny passed away, as there were no other family members or neighbours who attended, and so I never had an affiliation with that church besides the fact that I associated fashion with religion from a young age.

Mummy or my neighbour, Ms. Baugie, would take me to church on Saturday mornings, where I'd listen to Biblical stories and go to Sabbath School with my brother, sisters, friends, and neighbours. Nobody dressed as formally or properly as they had at the Baptist church. Gigantic hats weren't displayed upon women's heads. Yet the women wore long skirts or dresses below their knees, and no makeup or jewelry. When I asked Mummy about the dress code, she told me, "It's a requirement of the church to show respect to our community and to God." I nodded, as the answer did make sense to me, and so I started wearing my long formal skirt to church too.

It was fun to not only listen to Biblical stories and learn about religion, but to also have a positive association with the Bible, and learn new songs with my siblings, from a young age. After story time came my least favorite part – the pastor's sermon. I always felt sleepy during these sermons, and I would tune it out by resorting to daydreaming.

I vividly remember one sermon in particular where the pastor preached about how sinful it was to commit fornication or have a child out of wedlock. Questions flooded my mind, and I wanted to know what that meant. Initially I thought when two people loved each other they got married, they had children and that was the end of it. I did not realize couples got involved outside of marriage or that it was considered sinful by the church until then. When I began to understand for myself, I thought to myself that the church contradicted itself as I witnessed the same person relaying these messages behaving inappropriately with a married church member.

I felt we were being told one thing, while the actual practice was completely different from what was being preached, it was as if rules and regulations only applied only when it was convenient. There were times the preacher would stare at people and start berating them for drinking Pepsi. I felt really uncomfortable watching this. Instead of having a positive message to share with the congregants, I constantly felt as though the sermons weren't supportive. In fact, I felt like they weren't even meant to be encouraging. As a young girl, I felt attacked for being a female, for desiring nice things or for visualizing a life outside of the church or society's norm. It was as if the pastor was pointing a finger at each of us, ensuring we focused on our shortfalls rather than our talents. As I became a teenager, I had disagreements with Mummy about attending church.

Every Saturday morning, she'd barge into my room and ask, "Why aren't you dressed yet, Sandy?" I knew church was important to her, yet I couldn't muster the energy to attend, only to feel like I was being attacked once again. I was thirteen years old by then and had already been through strife in my life – bullies had picked on me, and I didn't need religion to do the same.

I groaned underneath the sheets, murmuring, "I'm not going, Mummy."

I heard her sighing, a tell-tale sign that she was about to cave into my demands, as usual.

"Okay, Sandy," she said. "Please, let's all go as a family, and then I promise you can have time with your cousins to swim."

She knew how much I loved to swim and be outside, but she also knew my views on the pastor and his sermons at this point. It bothered me that when I asked her questions, she just assumed the pastor knew more than she did; she believed in him wholeheartedly, whereas I did not. I continued to go to church until the first year after high school. At this point I was able to use the excuse of studying and doing homework to avoid church. Later on in my life, I would find a church that accepted me, and everyone else, as they were without judgment.

Chapter 6

Bullying at School

When I was still in my primary years of school, my private prep school, which was less than a mile from my house, permanently closed due to a lack of funding. I was devastated when I found out I would need to transfer into a different school. It was the beginning of my first year attending a public all-age school and my first experience being bullied. I felt alienated and isolated.

In Jamaica at the time, there were no geographic boundaries in choosing a school. Though we resided in the parish of St. Mary, my parents decided to send us to school in the adjoining parish of Portland, just four miles east of our home. My father had to drive his Ford Escort past the school on his way to work in the mornings, so he dropped us off at school in the mornings.

While sitting at my narrow wooden desk in class, I would feel my hair, in one long braid, being tugged and dragged. My friends Geraldine and Sophie would always tell me to ignore them as they were just envious of my hair.

"Please, I just want to do my schoolwork in peace, please stop pulling my hair," I pleaded with them.

"You are a coolie gal," they would exclaim to my olive brown face. The other girls in class, except for Geraldine and Sophie, all had much darker skin tone with short coarse hair. Their hair reminded me of my maternal grandmother, whom I adored. I would always comb and style her hair in different ways, and she would braid mine when she came to visit. Yet whenever she braided my hair, it would just unravel, and this memory came back to haunt me during this one year of public school; before, I did not put much thought into different hair textures as I only saw a sea of personalities, everyone with their own unique characteristics. I then realize there are others who will discriminate because of a slightly different skin tone, hair texture, financial status, culture or belief system – very small things which did not make much sense to me – all because of their inability to comprehend that there is only one human race; that colour, creed or religion does not matter as we are all human beings with our own individual sense of doing and understanding. We can choose to be around like-minded people with similar values, but this does not mean we should discriminate against those who are of different minds, value systems or appearances. We cannot all think and do the same.

Tears started to well up in my eyes, and the girls pointed at me, laughing.

"Coolie shit pon Callaloo and tun round nyam eh!" they shouted. I didn't really understand what that meant, but I understood they meant to demean me by uttering that statement. I so badly wanted to tell my parents, or my older brother but he no longer lived with us, or someone trustworthy who would listen to me. But if I did, I knew there would be repercussions. I soon learned that even if I tried telling a teacher, they wouldn't listen.

A memory came to my mind as the girls continued their taunting. A week beforehand, the principal, Ms. T, had lined everyone up in school and told us to put out our hands. I didn't know why we were doing this, but I always did what I was told by the adults in my life. The sting of the whip hit my hands hard, and a dark, red blood mark tattooed my wrist as tears came to my eyes. Ms. T only whipped me. All the other children, who didn't look like me, were spared. I felt like I was being punished for looking different, and nothing more. At eleven years old, I knew this was wrong, but I didn't know what to do about the situation. I knew if I stayed quiet and kept my head down, nose-deep in my books, then I would survive until it was time to leave the school.

Someone shifted in their iron chair, scraping the concrete floor after what seemed like eternity, and I came back to my present hell.

In Jamaica back then, a common entrance exam determined which students got to attend traditional high schools. When the exam results were published, my name was nowhere to be found. It was as if I didn't exist, and my hard work – I had studied for months – meant nothing at all. I had assumed I failed, even though there was no possibility of that, since I had always received straight As.

Luckily, my father became involved in the situation. After all, I was still a child, and though I liked to think I was entirely independent, I still needed my parents, especially in times of crises.

When my father spoke to the school, he was told that several exam papers were "mixed up," and I would need to repeat the sixth grade, study once again, and take the exam. He relayed this news to me, and I sat there, shattered and in disbelief.

"Daddy, please, I cannot go back to that school for another year!" I pleaded with him. "Please, this is the biggest thing I will ever ask for, I won't be able to last another year in that environment. The students and teachers are mean to me every single day. It's a nightmare. I need to go to a different school and experience school in a different way. I'll do anything, even wash the dishes every day for the rest of my life. I cannot stay another year to take the exam, I will not survive!"

I started crying in front of him, something I've rarely done in my life.

He looked at me compassionately with sad, brown eyes, deep in thought.

"Sandy, I'll talk with the high school. We'll stick with our plan. Don't you worry, my daughter. We will find a solution." He smiled, patted me on the shoulder, and walked away. I felt comforted knowing he was so nonchalant about the whole affair.

The next day, he spoke to the principal of the high school I wanted to attend. To this day, I have no idea how my daddy finagled a meeting with this principal, but he did. They had me take a test, after which the principal made a space for me at the school.

Relief was an understatement.

I felt as if I had won the lottery of lotteries.

When my father told me the good news, I felt very proud to have such a father, and for the first time that year, a happy grin brightened my face. I couldn't wait for high school to start. I had worked so hard academically. The social aspect of school was never a priority for me, as I didn't care about having a boyfriend, or even close friends. I had my family and my books, and those were enough for me. I was always placed at the top of my class; math and English were my favorite subjects. By the time I was thirteen years old, I had already read Charles Dickens, Jane Austen, and hundreds of other authors' work within various genres. Books were a way I could have alone time. With a huge family, neighbours and relatives stopping by all of the time, and a large church community, I was surrounded by people constantly. Though I loved my family and my community, I needed my solitude. From a young age, I knew I needed to find time to be with my inner thoughts to truly have peace within myself, and to have peace with my surroundings. Books gave me that superpower. Books allowed me to live freely through so many characters, and I learned so much about who I wanted to become.

Chapter 7

Driving with Daddy

"Daddy! Are you ready to go?"

I had my backpack by our front door, and I tucked away the lunch money Mummy gave me in the side pocket of my uniform. My father had recently been promoted to Parish Manager for Portland, as he worked for the National Water Commission. His office was based in Port Antonio, where my high school was located. My father and I spent countless hours in the car driving to Port Antonio and back to Markingstone; it was a small district outside of Annotto Bay in St. Mary with very limited traffic, yet the drive still took forty-five minutes each way. By this time, my father had changed his car to a Honda Accord. I didn't care about waking up at 5 a.m. daily for school. I was excited about the prospect of not being picked on daily, and I also looked forward to spending extra time with my father.

"Okay Sandy, time to go," he called out to me.

After about fifteen minutes of driving, we turned off into a housing scheme. I stayed quiet and observed instead of asking questions, since that was my nature.

We pulled up to a small rectangular house, and a man attired in a light blue colored bush jacket and grey pants entered our car.

"Hello," he said nonchalantly. "Thanks for the ride, Daniel."

"It's no problem," Daddy said to him with his eyes on the road. "It wasn't out of our way."

Just then, Mr. Senior suddenly noticed me out of the corner of his eye.

"Oh! Didn't see you there, Sandy."

How does he know my nickname? I thought to myself.

He smiled and started chatting with Daddy about their jobs at the National Water Commission. Daddy was always mild-mannered, and he never really put on a show for anyone. When he walked into a room, he became the highlight and you could see the respect that everyone had for him, however he was completely unaware. He was kind and generous to everyone and it showed in how he related to those he came in contact with, and I admired that about him. "So senior, how are the operations going at the plant?"

"Oh, fine," Mr. Senior said. "With all the recent upgrades and the resizing of the pipeline we were able to increase our overall supply since the demand is expanding, which is always a good thing."

The National Water Commission, according to its website, produces more than 90% of Jamaica's total potable water supply from a network of more than 160 underground wells, over 116 river sources (via water treatment plants) and 147 springs. About 30% of the water abstracted in Jamaica is used to meet the demand for potable water and the remaining 70% is used for irrigation.

I also learned that about 70% of Jamaica's population is supplied via house connections from the National Water Commission, and the remaining 30% obtains water from standpipes, wayside tanks, water trucks, rainwater catchment tanks, community catchment tanks, and direct access to rivers and streams.

Before my drives with Daddy, I took the act of drinking pure, delicious water for granted. I had never realized the extent to which people in Jamaica worked in order to ensure its citizens were provided with clean drinking water.

"Now that's progress," Daddy said matter of factly, "but didn't you say in the management meeting the other day that our demand is down?"

"Oh, no, that wasn't me," said Mr. Senior, lowering his head. I would soon learn that body language was a key indicator of whether or not someone was telling the truth.

"Anyways, how's school, Sandy?"

"Fine," I remarked casually, not wanting to interrupt their important business conversation. I never spoke unless I was asked a direct question. Throughout high school, I was quiet and reserved. I kept my head down, buried in piles of books, usually novels, always listening intently.

I did fairly average academically. While I was hungry to learn, I didn't care to study more than I needed to. I listened to my teachers, and I observed what was happening around me without appearing attentive. I always considered myself an observer, and this continued throughout high school. My grades remained average, and I was happy with them. I preferred to listen and understand new information on my own terms; I didn't feel as though I needed to read a textbook in order to fully comprehend any subject. To this day, I would rather figure out how to put something together by myself rather than read the manual.

My father was always my ultimate protector. He would tell my mother, "Babs, don't make Sandy wash any plates, she needs to spend her time reading her books!" Yet my siblings didn't get the same treatment as they misbehaved a lot. Daddy wanted me to go and study. He believed in me. Yet I took advantage of his kindness and pretended to study while reading my mystery novels. At this point, thankfully, Aunt Ruthcid had moved away and was living in New York City, so she wasn't able to come into my room and demand that I study or tell my parents I wasn't really studying, which she would have done if she had still been living with us. I knew I wouldn't have gotten away with not "studying" for this long had she been here, and I was grateful that I didn't have to deal with her put downs and sarcasm.

"You're in Form 4 now, correct?" Mr. Senior asked, bringing me back to the present.

"Yes, that's right."

In Jamaica, students have a right to choose between six to ten subjects to study in order to take the Caribbean Examination Council's or the GCE O-Level examinations.

"What are you leaning towards?" asked Mr. Senior.

"I really like the arts, including History and Art," I said slowly, "but I enjoy learning about business from Daddy."

Mr. Senior chuckled.

"Keep up the good work and the good attitude, kiddo, and don't let anyone else tell you what subjects to take. Follow your gut."

I nodded as Mr. Senior and Daddy went back to their conversation about the upgrade of the water distribution network, and I listened intently.

Unlike other high schoolers, particularly girls, I wasn't concerned about hanging with my friends or boys. In first form, my best friend at the time, Geraldine, started high school alongside me, but we had a falling out due to me not having the patience to wait while she stopped and chatted with every boy that called to her. We would walk together from school occasionally, and she would stop to chat with a boy, while I continued on to my intended destination. I didn't care to wait for her, because I wanted to do my schoolwork and learn more from Daddy. Geraldine eventually left the school after the first year as she was unable to keep up with the academic rigor, and we lost touch with each other after that.

Even though boys weren't a priority, I learned about relationships through books as I grew up. In my early years, I loved reading the stories of Cinderella, Rapunzel, Sleeping Beauty and countless others with their endings of happily ever after's. After that I started reading novels by Sidney Sheldon, Nora Roberts, VC

Andrews, James Patterson and many more. I also used to watch the Sunday classics on Jamaica Broadcasting Corporation, or JBC TV (owned by Radio Jamaica Rediffusion [RJR] as of 1997) every Sunday morning at 10 a.m. Later on, I added romance novels to the list of books I consumed on a regular basis.

Besides my parents, neighbours, and observing other couples, reading these stories were my only references to what falling in love and getting married would be like. I sometimes fantasized about my own Prince Charming, but in reality, I wasn't looking for my Prince Charming in high school.

Chapter 8

A Heart for Business

After Daddy dropped me off at school in the mornings, I would listen keenly to the teacher speaking in class and take notes, but I rarely ever referred back to those notes. Whenever I had break time or was done with my class work, I buried my head in books and magazines. I particularly found the era during and after World War II intriguing. Reading about new and interesting subjects was the only thing that got me through school. I had developed a general dislike for school and though high school was better, I still struggled with fitting in, and I realized I had no desire to. I was always well behaved, very disciplined, and extremely organized in my thinking and the portrayal of myself. I was constantly over-thinking and analyzing everything, though I did not share my thoughts openly with anyone. I psychoanalyzed my teachers, not knowing that's what I was doing at the time. I realized that a greater portion of my teachers did not have a passion for teaching, and this was displayed by the amount of time they did not show up to teach the class. When they did appear, they were disgruntled with the world and took it out on the students. Therefore, I decided that I would not pursue a career I was not passionate about, but if I did, I would still give it my best.

I attended Titchfield High School in Port Antonio. The school compound was originally a Spanish fort, built during the time when the Spaniards colonized Jamaica. After the British conquered the Spanish in 1655, the fort was later converted to a school. The school facility consisted of multiple buildings, including three main buildings with large corridors, standing at two floors high and overlooking the play field to the south and the Port Antonio natural Harbour to the west, the horizon to the north and the eastern harbour gazing over the bay to the Folly ruins. Just west of the main building there was a small white sand beach where I would sometimes remove my shoes and walk the shore during the lunch hour, looking across at Navy Island, once owned by the famous movie star Errol Flynn. There were other smaller detached buildings and the canons between the barrack walls were still present. This was my favorite part about school. The landscape semi-circled by the Caribbean Sea and getting to watch the ships and fishing boats up close sailing through the Harbour.

In town, there was a pharmacy called Square Deal Pharmacy which was owned by our family doctor – Dr Poyser. I religiously stopped at the pharmacy after school, whether I was walking to my father's office, getting a ride with my father or taking the bus home. That's where they had a magazine and book stand. Instead of buying lunch with my $100 Jamaican dollars daily, I saved it. I would buy Time magazine, The Economist, Forbes, and Seventeen to read. I also bought National Geographic and How Things Work; at one point, even though I wasn't interested in airplanes, I purchased a book about planes and took it to my two younger brothers, who didn't even look at the book.

I preferred to spend this money on learning material from the outside world versus eating. I figured I could always eat later in the day. I would always look forward to my mummy's dinner, often daydreaming about going home and eating her food. By the time I got home I would be starving, which made my mother's cooking even tastier, and I was even more grateful for her delicious meals. My favorite dish at the time was stewed peas served with steamed white rice. Stewed peas is a hearty island stew made with red peas and meat and cooked in a coconut milk broth, and seasoned with Jamaican spices including pimento, which gives the dish its distinct flavor.

Occasionally, Daddy would send someone to pick me up after school. When I was not picked up, it took about fifteen minutes to walk from school to the main square of the town. I had to walk up a hill then down the hill, then it took another fifteen minutes to get to my dad's office. There were two roads – the top road and bottom road. The bottom road was quite scenic along the seaside with a view of the bay and the easier road as it descended all the way. However, I always chose the top road, as it was less lonely with buildings lining both sides of the street; I just felt safer walking that route even though I had to walk up the hill and then down.

At Daddy's workplace, I nibbled on jerk chicken or pork – a daily treat I looked forward to after school, since I hadn't eaten anything at that point since breakfast. When I finished eating, I would sit at a huge box adjacent to my father's desk, make some room and complete my schoolwork. Having a specific environment to do my work was never on the table for me, because I never had the option. My only choices were to do my school assignment at Daddy's office in this nook, or not do my homework until way past dinnertime when I was at home and surrounded by raucous noise from my younger siblings in the evenings.

Accomplishing tasks like my schoolwork earlier in the day left me feeling rejuvenated, and, while I did like some of my schoolwork, I actually enjoyed learning more about Daddy's job. When I completed my school assignments daily, I volunteered in Daddy's office – and loved every single minute. I was always an inquisitive child, and my questioning nature didn't stop in high school. In fact, I was eager to learn more. I had a desire to understand what my father did every day for work, and how work played an integral part of not only his life, but also our family's life. Through simple tasks like typing, arranging files, and anything else his secretary Miss Wright would allow me to do, I thoroughly enjoyed listening to and being around the office environment. I heard and witnessed conversations daily about office management, office politics, customer issues, and so much more. I stayed in my little corner and occasionally eavesdropped when Daddy had meetings in his office. I felt the urge to understand every business-related task my dad was doing. My exposure to the world of commerce, operations, maintenance, and the public water supply was prominent. While at the office, I happily did what was asked of me, unlike other kids I witnessed there. Once, I saw another teenager a few years older than me complaining when his mother asked him to organize some paper on her desk.

"I can't help with that right now!" he exclaimed.

I found this attitude to be reprehensible and downright disrespectful. I swore to myself that I would never react with such an ill-mannered attitude in any situation, especially if it was work; whether it was volunteering at Daddy's office or any job I had as an adult.

At times, I would accompany Daddy on visits to water treatment plants across the parish, from the Charlestown plant in Buff Bay to Grants Level east of Port Antonio, where I would observe how the water distribution system worked. I learned the entire mapping of the water distribution system for the parish of Portland by merely observing and listening. I watched, listened, and learned, absorbing as much knowledge as possible, like a sponge soaking up water. I was fascinated by the large pumps with pressure tanks, the reservoirs and the large pipelines which allowed water to be distributed across the parish and into the pipes of almost every household.

During Christmastime one year, my parents took me along to a holiday party. I was the only one of my siblings to ever be taken along to one of these momentous parties, and I believe this was due to my calm behavior, contrary to my siblings who tended to be more on the hyperactive side. Though I was only fourteen years old, I found myself in discussions about water treatment, Jamaica's water distribution system, current affairs, and a host of other topics.

Daddy's coworkers would say to him, "You must be so proud of your daughter!" after having conversed with me for only a short time. At the time, I didn't quite understand why my parents would be "so proud of me." Wasn't I just a normal teenager who liked observing and a little more on the inquisitive side? Wasn't I just my father's daughter at work? I didn't think I did, or said, anything extraordinary; as a matter of fact, I had very little confidence in my abilities. I simply assumed these adults were being extra kind to me because I was my father's daughter. I was in high school, and my academic performance was average, however I came to realize that I had above-average common sense. So, though I looked at life from a real-world perspective, I started imagining my ideal world; a world where my thoughts would be the driver in achieving my reality.

I later recognized that my father's colleagues weren't just being nice. They saw my abilities and were impressed with my knowledge and astuteness. My peers weren't having these discussions at grown up parties. They were talking about boys, crushes, and gossiping about one another in their own meeting spaces. They would discuss the latest fashion and makeup trends, from what I observed during the school day. But these topics were of secondary interest to me. I was mostly interested in learning more about business operations. From this point on, I had a desire to start my own business one day when I became an adult, though I wasn't quite sure in which industry, and I had never even met a female CEO. It even crossed my mind that one day I could start a private water company, but this thought was pushed back deep into my subconscious.

Having these discussions about business at office parties was much more interesting to me than discussing any "normal" fourteen-year-old topics. I didn't want, or need, the distraction of boys. Besides, I had my reading, schoolwork, and volunteering to keep me busy. Not to say I didn't develop any crushes – I did – but I warded off the boys with my power to ignore, my sharp tongue, and targeted antisocial attitude. I couldn't bring myself to want this for myself, despite having this fantasy of finding my Prince Charming like in the fairy tales I consumed in my earlier years. I saw many teenagers get caught up in relationships too soon and they often ended up becoming teenage moms; I was not interested in becoming another statistic, so I kept my distance when it came to boys. I later understood that the adults around me saw a spark within me that I didn't see within myself until many years later.

*

When I was in the middle of my Fourth Form school year, equivalent to 10th grade, I became much more interested in pursuing business subjects. Though I still enjoyed learning about art, and even some science, volunteering at Daddy's office in high school spurred me into wanting to learn more about how I could step into Daddy's shoes and become a manager. Even though I didn't see many women in leadership positions at Daddy's company, there was a small voice inside my head that continually asked, "Why not me? Why can't I learn this material?" And so, I did, starting with my remaining years in high school, but it was not without repercussions.

When I entered Fifth Form, or 11th grade, I switched to a different Fifth Form which focused on business subjects. I am uncertain whether this was the educational-system norm in Jamaica, however, I asked and was transferred. All the business subjects were mandatory in this new class, so I ended up giving up History and Art which I loved and continued Human and Social Biology as an elective because I also enjoyed science and learning about the human body. Pursuing a business course of study in Jamaica, to most people, meant that I would end up as a clerical staff worker in some random office. Becoming a doctor, a lawyer, teacher, or nurse were of high stature, which is why my peers saw my decision as a downgrade.

One day, a classmate and friend, Shernette, told me some students were saying I was demoted upon finding out I was transferred to a business class.

"Why in the world would you do this to yourself, S?" Shernette said to me, looking confused. "I wouldn't do what you did. I'll continue taking History, Biology, and a host of other subjects so I can go to England where my father lives and attend college and become a teacher." She spoke as if business subjects were not considered real subjects.

Another classmate, Rose-Ann, informed me that she would be a lawyer, and anyone who didn't want to be a lawyer or a doctor was an idiot.

"These debate classes will help me do what I'm meant to do," she said proudly to me along the corridor when I was minding my own business.

I listened intently, though I never asked anyone for their opinions. I never even asked my own parents. When I decided to pursue something for myself, I accepted that it was common to receive negative feedback from outsiders who didn't quite understand my decisions, so I did not hold it against them, nor did I care for their opinions. Hearing these comments made me grow stronger. I built up my confidence and my resilience muscles in 11th grade by not letting anyone else tell me which subjects would be "helpful for my career," considering no one giving this advice would live my life for me. By then, I already understood I was responsible for my own life, and for my own career. I started to understand what Daddy's colleagues saw in me just two years prior.

Chapter 9

Acceptance as a Teenager

A month after I celebrated my fifteenth birthday, I was sitting with my beloved grandfather, Big Papa, on the verandah outside my parents' home. I was taking a break from schoolwork, watching the waves of the sea rise and fall, hearing nature's echo from the comfort of my home. Big Papa and I usually sat in silence, and we would sip his protein juice, the same one he made when I was six years old. Suddenly, he turned to me with a serious expression and caught my eyes.

"I wish I could live to see you become the greatest person you will become." He stared at me with his wide, brown eyes. The wrinkles on his face had become more prominent over the past several months, yet I hadn't noticed until this very moment.

"Big Papa, why are you saying this? We have plans to go fishing tomorrow, and then we'll get ice cream, right?"

He casually smiled and nodded, taking a sip of his protein shake. He knew we wouldn't be going but couldn't bring himself to tell me at that time. He would no longer be here by then.

Sometimes sitting in silence is an act of courage in itself. In this case, that's what my grandfather chose to do. He sat in silence until he was having trouble breathing. He rocked forward in his favorite chair, slowly slumping over, not able to control his physical movements.

"Big Papa! Stay with me!" I stood up and rushed over to him immediately. "Help, please help me!" I shouted.

He reached out and grabbed the inside of my left elbow. I can still feel his warm, gentle touch on my skin to this day.

He looked up at me lovingly and said his last words, "Goodbye, my special granddaughter."

"No no no!" I screamed vehemently. "Stay. With. Me."

I hadn't realized that he had already closed his eyes. He was ready to be with Granny.

By the time anyone else had arrived, Big Papa had passed away. I cried myself to sleep that night, burying my face in pillows and not allowing anyone to approach me. I needed to grieve in my own way, and this was almost, in a way, a tougher loss than when Granny passed away. As we grow older, we experience loss and grief in profoundly different ways. At six years old, I had somewhat of an understanding that I wouldn't see Granny again. But at fifteen years old, I had developed so many more memories with Grandpa. Whenever we would get ice cream on Sundays, he would always order vanilla ice cream cake. Even though my favorite is chocolate ice cream, I can't go to an ice cream store without getting vanilla ice cream cake in memory of Big Papa.

*

My teenage years were that of a normal teenager. There were family outings on Sundays when my father would pack all six of us in the car and drive us to a beach in another parish or to visit a relative where they were having an Indian celebration and we would eat an array of Indian dishes, listen to Indian music and learn Indian dance. At Christmastime, Daddy would take us into the city capital of Kingston on Christmas Eve, and he would buy each one of us two new toys each and two suits of new clothes. My summer holidays were filled with excursions to my father's farm where I, along with my siblings, cousins and friends, fished in the ponds and swam and frolicked all day in the river. We roasted fish and jangas. We ate cantaloupe, guavas, melon, and ripe bananas and drank coconut water which was in abundance on the farm. The farm was about two and a half miles from my home, so I had to ride my bicycle along with my siblings to get there. My sister and I rode pink BMX bikes while my two brothers rode black BMX bikes. My two younger siblings were not allowed to go with us because they were too young and that would mean we would constantly have to be babysitting them if they went with us. My childhood memories were happy and exciting. I recall this one time we were up by our friends' home by Iteborale where we always hung out with our neighbourhood friends. We would ride up an incline then ride down. On one such occasion after riding down, I was parked at the bottom of the incline speaking to some of my friends when I heard shouting. I looked up and saw my youngest sister on my little brother's bike, it was coming much too fast; her little legs were not even long enough to touch the ground and she did not know how to slow down or break. If she did not stop, she would collide with a barbed wire fence or an oncoming vehicle. I instantly started riding toward her then I jumped off my bike and stood in front of the oncoming bike, holding out my hands towards the bars to stop it. I managed to stop the bike but not without both of us falling, both my knees hitting the pavement as the bicycle tilted to one side. My little sister ended up with a bruised knee, and both my knees and the palm of my hands were bruised and bleeding. That was the first time I had to be courageous and decisive, and it led to me embracing a sense of responsibility towards my younger siblings. I began to fully understand my role as an older sister.

When I ventured away from home and people started complimenting me on my appearance and smile, I thought they were being pretentious. I became distrustful and timid. After all, why would I believe strangers over my own aunt? It was when I moved away from home and started appreciating that I was actually a kind-hearted person, and nothing was wrong with me, that I started recognizing that people were complimenting me based on their individual perceptions and the genuineness they detected in me. I learned to respect and appreciate others' authenticity which led me to accepting myself and my God-given talents. I could sew, paint, draw, swim, write poems, sing, solve mysteries and puzzles, do hairstyles, cook and so much more. I started telling myself I was beautiful, brilliant and I could do whatever I put my mind to. I slowly learned to love and accept myself and who I was becoming.

Chapter 10

Meeting Him

I halted in my tracks when I saw him.

I was sixteen years old, and I had never laid eyes on a more handsome man in my life. I felt a strange urge to be close to him. I felt a warmth that I had never in my life experienced before. But it was only for a moment, and I shook my head, bringing myself back to reality.

A year later, I saw him again. He was the nephew of Daddy's friend, and we would bump into each other occasionally at family cookouts. After many occasions of smiling at him and shying away from his flirtatious stare, he finally walked over to me one day.

"Hey, I hear you like to swim."

He brought a water coconut and offered it to me; I was thirsty after coming from a swim in the nearby river, so I gladly accepted it.

I looked up and smiled at him. I had never before been approached in this way by a boy, or a man, and I wasn't sure of the protocol. I didn't know what to say, or what not to say, so I stood there, observing and smiling.

"My name is Devon." He smiled at me. His jet-black, smooth hair was brushed back while falling to the side, and he wore a white-coloured polo shirt, perfectly crisp and ironed. I was still in my swimsuit from earlier in the day but was wearing generous coverup over it, so I felt presentable enough.

"So, what's your name?"

"Sandy."

"Wow, how pretty. And not just the name."

I smiled, blushed and felt awkward at the attention.

He's really cute, I thought.

But then I noticed a shiny gold band on his ring finger. On his left hand.

Maybe he's not married? I questioned what I saw. *Why would he flirt with me at a party with both our families here? And where is his wife? Wouldn't she be here?*

"Listen, my job takes me away a lot," he said, looking me in the eyes. "I'm a marine navigator and I work on a chemical tanker at sea. But I want to see you again."

He wrote down a number on a piece of carton he tore from a box and handed it to me. He gave me a blank piece as well.

"Write down your number, and I'll call you."

There was that mischievous smile again. Gosh, was he handsome!

*

Months later, I saw Devon taking pictures at my high school graduation, and I knew he had snapped a photo of me. He smiled, staring at me – his usual form of saying hello from afar. After the ceremony, I posed for a few more photos, yet instead of thinking about my accomplishments, I was only thinking about Devon. I had found out he was, indeed, still married, and I didn't know what to do about these unnatural and strange feelings of lust I had developed for him over the past few months.

He approached me and said, "Congratulations, grad!"

"Devon," I whispered. "I'm not sure why you snapped a photo of me, and why you're even here… listen, I know you're married."

I took a step back in my white heels, almost tripping over in my light blue dress.

He took my hands in his, but not before glancing around the room to see who was watching us.

"Sandy," he said in a serious tone of voice. "I'm getting a divorce. I promise. It's not working out. All I can think of is you… My cousin Georgia is one of the graduates, so she asked me to come and take pictures of her graduating."

I smiled, unsure of what to do with this newfound semi-relationship, and the new feelings I was experiencing.

The previous week, I had told a fellow schoolmate that I would attend the high school graduation party with him at the

Rafters Rest by the Rio Grande, a hotel by the Rio Grande riverbank west of Port Antonio.

I worked up the nerve to ask Devon if he'd like to go with me, completely disregarding the fact that I had already committed to going with someone else.

"Sorry." His tone of voice changed drastically from just a minute prior. He didn't sound as kind, or as warm-hearted. "I gotta get to work actually. Have fun though and talk soon."

He turned around, leaving me in an icy energy surrounding the space where I stood. Yet this nagging feeling kept tugging at my chest, wanting Devon for myself.

I was too sad to attend the party, and I didn't bother letting my previous date know I wasn't going to attend. It wasn't worth the effort, as I was in such a negative headspace at this point. As a teenager, I was never interested in parties, and I didn't feel like celebrating the achievement of graduating high school. My fears about the future surpassed any positive feelings I had about leaving high school. At the time, I didn't think, "Wow, I did it! I graduated high school!" Instead, I thought, "I graduated high school... I'm an adult now. Where do I go from here?" The anxious thoughts overwhelmed in my mind. Besides, the fact that Devon couldn't accompany me, and that Daddy was unable to attend my graduation ceremony, made the whole ordeal less inviting. Daddy was always a huge support, but business took him away from me at a time I needed him the most. It wasn't worth the effort of putting on a fake smile and attending a party where I couldn't even showcase all my emotions, so I opted out.

Chapter 11

Yearning to Learn

Though I had technically graduated from high school, I returned to pursue some additional classes for pre-sixth form. I did not have the requisite subjects to go straight to sixth form after missing a few of my exams due to a minor accident I experienced.

External exams had started that week and I stood outside, waiting to catch the bus. It halted to a stop, and I saw that it was packed, as per usual, with the conductor hanging out the door. I stepped up, but before I could hold on to something, the bus drove off and I fell off and onto the street. By the time I realized what had happened, my mouth had sand in it, and I could taste blood. The impact of the bus speeding away kicked up the dirt, and my teeth grazed the inside of my lip. My backpack is what saved me from hitting my head. The experience of taking the bus for me was horrible, even before this incident occurred. The buses were always packed like sardines and most times I had to stand for the whole journey which was more than an hour. After high school, I decided I would never ever take another bus in my life. I would make sure that I would work to earn enough money so I could buy myself a car.

The accident caused me to miss my Caribbean Examination Council exams which I was to sit that day and the next; added to this, my performance on the exams I completed were average. At home, my father went to work overseas, which was burdensome for my mother, who suddenly became the head of the household. I could chalk up my average performance on the exams I did complete to challenging times in my family life, but the simple fact was that I did not study, and I did not care to study as I lacked the commitment, telling myself the textbooks were uninteresting and monotonous.

Months later, I would attend the Institute of Computer Technology in California with the help of my brother and my uncle. Yet a quarter of the way through the programme, I realized I needed to pursue business. I earned a Certificate in Micro-Computerized Accounting after a year of study and hard work, then got into a business management program, where I later completed an Associates Degree in Business Business Management.

I had a thirst for knowledge that may have been unattainable for some, yet I knew in my heart I could manage these high expectations for myself. I used to say aloud, "If this doesn't work, there will always be something else that will." This attitude is what drove me to become successful at multiple endeavors throughout my life which also led to me earning a Bachelor of Science Degree in Business Administration from the University of Phoenix and later a Master of Law Degree from the University of Cumbria.

Part 2:
Elizabeth

Chapter 12

Wellness Check

I pulled a ripe scotch bonnet pepper off a tree, examining it. Yet today, the yellow, earthy scent of the pepper sent my nostrils flying, and an overwhelming sense of nausea and dizziness came over me.

"What's wrong?" my father asked, concerned. I could see the worry on his face which suggested I looked like how I was feeling – which was really awful.

I felt the blood rushing to my face, and I sank low to the ground, feeling the brown, damp soil underneath my fingernails.

"I'm... not sure... Daddy," I said, gasping for air and trying to hold myself together.

"Go to the pick-up and sit for a while. I will get you some coconut water, then take you home."

My father was always telling me to eat food or drink something, even though I was twenty years old. He meant well – this was his language of showing love and affection towards me, his eldest daughter.

As I slowly walked back to the pick-up truck, I looked over and saw the refreshing blue-green river flowing effortlessly to meet the Caribbean Sea, the offspring of the North Atlantic Ocean. The crisp water expanded beyond the horizon in a similar way to the Pacific Ocean which at a glance seemed never ending. I had only left California several months ago, with my certificate in Micro-Computerized Accounting.

Though I sometimes missed the energetic pace of California, I was so happy to be home, spending time with my family and enjoying the sunny, clear skies and cool sea breeze. I particularly loved chatting with my father about the new crops we were planting just before spring. Yet, over the past few weeks, I hadn't felt much like myself. Nausea overwhelmed me. The mere thought of meat made me run to the bathroom.

Maybe I should see a doctor. Something isn't right.

Devon came to visit that evening, and I told him that I had made a doctor's appointment in Kingston. I wanted him – needed him – to accompany me. In the back of my mind, I knew there was the possibility of me being pregnant. Even though I was on the pill, sometimes I would forget to take it and try to play catch up, which ultimately did not work.

At the appointment, the doctor confirmed I was nine weeks pregnant.

I had mixed feelings as I was not married, did not have a stable income and I was still living with my parents. My relationship with Devon at the time was difficult as I had recently found out that he was fooling around with a girl who attended my former high school. I was really troubled, considering the predicament I found myself in, as our relationship had almost ended, and he was trying to patch things up with me. My moral compass only allowed one choice and that was to have my baby, so even though I was heartbroken, I chose to try to make our relationship work. I was still in love with Devon, and now we were going to have a baby together. I did wrestle with my value system, though, since Devon and I weren't yet married. The church made a mockery of women like me – young women who found themselves in this situation without a wedding band. Yet both of my parents were supportive. I eventually stopped working in Kingston and moved back into my parents' house in St. Mary fulltime.

Besides being handsome and charming, Devon was practical and hardworking. He had a talent for constructing buildings, so he eventually sold all the assets he had accumulated over the years to raise enough funds to partner with his mother and brother to pursue constructing a guesthouse, while I became an expectant mother. I did not discuss any future plans with Devon at the time, but deep down, all I wanted was to marry him, have his children and own our own home. I gave no thought to how this would be achieved, though. Growing up, I saw my father going to work and supporting his family with his earnings while my mother took care of the home and family, so naturally, this was the expected norm for me on the surface. My teenage dreams of becoming a female CEO were buried even further into my subconscious mind.

*

I was seven months pregnant when I started feeling the baby kicking continuously. I felt the weight of the baby pushing up into my chest and against the right side of my belly in a strange, tightening sensation. I called my doctor and explained how I felt, and she told me to go to the hospital which was an hour and a half away.

When I arrived at the hospital, I explained that my doctor had told me to come, and I asked the receptionist to call my doctor and let her know I was there. I sat quietly and waited for two hours, growing more uncomfortable by the minute with on-and-off shooting pains. Now, I wish I had spoken up sooner, but I was in so much pain – and so young and naïve – and I really thought my doctor would be there for me. A nurse passed by and looked at me, concern brewing in her eyes. She stopped and asked me if I was okay. I explained I was waiting to see the doctor who was on her way, supposedly, even though it had been two hours at this point. She went over to the receptionist and made a call, and another nurse came out and they took me to a room and had me lie on the bed. They tried to listen to the baby's heartbeat which seemed to be fading, then I remember them speaking very fast and rushing me into the operating room. I vaguely remember seeing the doctor standing over me fully garbed, and then a nurse was inserting a needle into my wrist. She spoke to the doctor and the other medical professionals in hushed whispers, and did not see that the connection from the needle to the tube fell off and blood was spurting out. I tried to get their attention by moving my mouth and hands, yet a respirator was already over my mouth and nose. I had no other advocates in the room besides myself. The doctor looked at me and remarked, "Poor thing, she's petrified." Hours later, I woke to see Devon sitting by my bedside; he looked relieved with a beaming smile on his face. All I wanted to know was whether our baby was okay.

"She's in the nursery," he whispered, holding my hand. "Go back to sleep now, get more rest." He took his phone out and began contacting our relatives, letting them know that I had woken up, and I drifted off to sleep once again.

It was dark when I awoke once again. Devon had left to go home. A nurse I didn't recognize came to visit me. She took my hand and said, "Okay Ms. Barker, let's try to walk to the restroom now. It will probably hurt but try to stand up straight and bear the pain. It'll get easier each time, I promise."

I squeezed her hand as I screeched in pain, forcing myself to focus on her words and get up from the bed, which I had laid on, at this point, for more than fifteen hours. When I was on my own two feet, I asked her insistently, "Where's the nursery? Point me there. I need to see my baby."

She nodded, expecting me to ask this question. She guided me past the room towards an outdoor corridor, where the nursery was several steps away.

I went to the window and saw the tiniest baby strapped in an incubator. A tube had been gently placed in her nose so she could breathe with help. Tears came to my eyes as I saw my daughter lying there. All I wanted to do was hold her and protect her at that moment, but I knew I couldn't do so. Not yet.

I walked back to my room empty-handed, forgetting the pain I was in momentarily while I let myself feel all of the emotions I was experiencing.

She shouldn't have come this early.

I felt as though I was in a dream-like state of mind. I had no clue how to navigate life post-partum, or how to look after a baby, let alone a baby with any medical issues. At the time, I still didn't quite know that Elizabeth would be a special child, requiring help around the clock.

The following morning, another nurse visited my room with a smile on her face.

"You're getting discharged today!" she said excitedly.

"What about my baby?" I asked.

"Oh, she needs to be here for a while longer."

I stared at her in disbelief. Rage presented itself, yet I sweetly said, "I'm not going home without my daughter."

She nodded and slowly walked away, taking my discharge papers with her.

On the third day of Elizabeth's life, she started breathing on her own, and we were both discharged together. Before we were, though, one of the doctors sat me down to explain what had happened to Elizabeth during delivery.

"When she was trying to turn," he started to say, "the umbilical cord got wrapped around her neck, cutting off her oxygen supply. We believe this has caused permanent brain damage. I'm so sorry."

He paused for just a moment before continuing. My heart sank to the bottom of my chest. I was barely an adult, and now I was responsible for taking care of my baby girl who apparently had suffered brain damage.

"It's possible she has a chromosome abnormality as well, but this requires some further testing …" He went on, discussing how Elizabeth would be developmentally delayed her whole life, but various sorts of therapies could help alleviate some of her delays.

I knew I'd love her no matter what, no matter who she was, or who she would become. Yet it was surreal to hold my small child on the way home, already knowing our journey wasn't starting out in a typical fashion.

I nursed Elizabeth, feeding her a half an ounce of formula at a time until she started sucking on her own. A love so strong came over me and I felt a great urge to protect her. It did not matter that I was sore and in pain from the C-section. Becoming a mother to Elizabeth changed my entire outlook on life. I wanted to protect her and give her everything and make her as comfortable as possible. She blossomed into a healthy baby, smiling all the time. However, her fine motor skills were not developing at the level they should be.

I soon came to terms with the fact that Elizabeth was going to be a special needs child all her life. All I could do for her at the time was to love and take care of her. I had to accept that she would always be dependent on me. She would be my baby forever.

*

Before Elizabeth turned one, Devon and I decided to get married on November 9, 1996. I wore a brown sleeveless dress with delicate white and purple flowers. Wearing a classic white dress wasn't important to me, as I had always done everything on my own terms. Devon didn't have a preference for what I wore either; he just wanted to be married to me. My hair was combed back into a neat but gorgeous bun that my mom and sisters helped put together. The pastor came to perform the ceremony in my parents' living room – I'm not sure whose idea it was at the time. My father, my mother, my three sisters, my niece, and Devon's best friend were in attendance; we had no intention of hosting a large gathering or reception. In Jamaica, the community usually comes together under the umbrella of "one love," where opening doors are an indication of an invitation rather than a paper or online version. We did not have the traditional wedding cake, the Sacred Cake, full of delicious spices, and soaked for weeks in the island's favorite – rum. Instead, we drank beef soup together and shared glasses of white wine. Devon and I occasionally reminisce about the simplicity of our wedding day and how much we loved that Elizabeth was able to be present for such a momentous occasion in our lives. I told myself that one day we would renew our vows and the traditional wedding cake would be included then. But the traditional wedding that I so desperately wanted – yearned for – never came to fruition.

*

I continued to play housewife after Devon and I got married. It was the role I was expected to play as a woman and young mother. Yet the toll it was taking on me became unbearable.

Elizabeth needed all different types of therapy and support, including speech, occupational, and physical. The cost alone was insurmountable, however we did not argue about money and finances like most married couples. We were both of humble economic means and I felt I needed to play a part in empowering our small family financially. Even though I saw my husband trying, I felt that I needed to help him as he seemed very stressed. I avoided conflict at all costs back then, always quietly trying to figure out the best course of action which would be beneficial to us all. Luckily, I was still able to live at my parents' house with Elizabeth, while Devon lived between his parents' house and mine. Over and over again, I softly indicated that I no longer wanted to stay at home but instead go out to find work. Deep inside my soul, this is what I truly wanted, though a large part of me felt guilty for wanting something for myself instead of constantly being there for Elizabeth. I was internalizing all these feelings I was having and constantly questioning my situation to the point of anxiety.

On a Thursday afternoon in December 1996, I had a full-blown panic attack. I couldn't control my breathing; I kept trying to inhale, but the air was sucked out of me before I felt it within my lungs. Existing in my parents' house as my child's caretaker wasn't enough for me; this was not the life I had envisioned for myself at those holiday parties years earlier, where I participated in adult conversations about real-world problems. When I realized I was hyperventilating, I attempted to calm myself down. Not one soul was around, besides Elizabeth, of course, and I soon realized that my mind was playing tricks on me. My thoughts were causing me to panic so drastically. I knew my thought patterns needed to change, yet I wasn't exactly sure how I would manage this change. I laid down on the cold terrazzo tiled floor and saw the sun peaking through the curtains. I closed my eyes and covered my erratically pounding heart with my hands.

1... 2... 3... 4...

I counted four counts in.

1... 2... 3... 4...

I held my breath for four seconds.

1... 2... 3... 4...

I slowly exhaled for four counts.

The sky looked gorgeous. The white clouds covered the blue sky in radiant light. Instead of only thinking about what I didn't have in my life, I started to consider what I did have and how lucky I was to be in this space. How lucky was I to have a gorgeous daughter, no matter what therapies she needed to develop into who she was meant to be? Hugging my knees, I sat upright, and a single tear fell onto my right cheekbone. But I didn't wipe it away. I let it linger, for all those negative thoughts needed to have a place to go, too. From that day on, I promised myself I would stop merely existing and start living the life I was meant to live. I knew I needed to be more than a housewife. I just didn't quite know where my journey would take me.

Chapter 13

A Conversion

A week after my full-blown panic attack, I sat on the quiet verandah, peacefully problem-solving a math equation while Elizabeth laid beside me, fast asleep. I wasn't currently in school, yet math had always been a source of comfort for me. Whenever I felt I needed to use my brain in a logical way, I could always rely on math to do the trick. Though I didn't necessarily have a fondness for math, I did have a fondness for finding solutions in general. And math helped me through some tough times as a young adult as at the time; it was what I had to resort to – to challenge myself.

I took a short break and looked up at the clear blue sky, admiring the clouds that filled the air. The sea was a beautiful blue; Elizabeth screeched for just a second, but the gorgeous, crystal blue sea soundscapes put her right back to sleep. Despite the warm, humid air, the slight breeze helped alleviate the sweat protruding from my temples. The branches on the bright floral Hibiscus plants in the yard swayed this way and that, and I breathed in a sense of love for the beautiful scenery surrounding me. Never once did I feel ungrateful for the life I was living, despite the challenges along the way.

I looked back down at my Math problem again, only to be interrupted by a stranger.

"Hey there."

Two young men approached the front gate to my yard with smiling faces, yet they were careful to not get too close. They were wearing matching white shirts with name tags, almost identical in size and stature. They were also both fair-skinned, a rare find in my Jamaican neighbourhood, so I automatically knew they weren't from around here. While I wasn't expecting someone to arrive at the house, particularly strangers, we were in a safe and friendly neighbourhood, so I wasn't too concerned.

I smiled back at them with a hand resting next to Elizabeth. I was her protector.

"How can I help you, young men?"

They stood awkwardly, about to speak when I interrupted them.

"Please come in, sit down. Let me get you some glasses of water."

I grabbed my sleeping baby girl and headed inside while the young men sat on the Verandah chairs and waited for me to return. I handed them both two glasses of chilled water then they proceeded to tell me what they were doing and who they were.

"We're missionaries of the Latter-Day Saints Church, ma'am," one of them said. "Have you heard of the Mormons?"

"Yes, I've heard of them but don't know much about them," I said honestly. Suddenly, I flashed back to when I lived in California after high school, which is where I met my first set of Mormon missionaries.

My one-bedroom apartment was situated in downtown Los Angeles just across the road from the St. Judes Shriners Hospital for Children on Geneva and Third street. I heard a knock at my door and slowly opened it to find two strangers. They stood outside my door awkwardly, trying to tell me something about how Joseph Smith was a prophet, but I didn't care. They offered me a copy of the Book of Mormon, and everything else they stated became garbled in my mind. At the time, I was not interested in spirituality or religion. I was only interested in finishing my college assignment which was due in two hours. I made some excuse as to why I needed to close my door and left them mid-sentence. Afterwards, I immediately threw the book in the trash. At the time, I thought the LDS church was contrary to the Holy Bible; my perception of Mormonism was clouded by others' perspectives at the time, who thought the Mormons were a polygamist cult.

But now, I had a new perception. I didn't really know how I felt about religion. It wasn't a priority for me – that much I knew. My priorities had shifted drastically once Elizabeth was born, and she was my number one.

"All we're here to do is hand you this."

He handed me the Book of Mormon. It felt lighter than the last one. I felt a presence surrounding me when I held it and allowed myself to feel again.

Was this a sense of belonging?

Was this what I was missing in my life?

"We're not here to force anyone," the other missionary stated. "We consider it our duty to ensure as many people as possible know about the message of Jesus Christ and that they read the scriptures. Would you be willing to take a look at these scriptures and pray about what you find?"

His serious blue eyes met my deep coffee-colored eyes. I stayed silent for another moment, and they looked around, first at Elizabeth, then glimpsed past the open door into the house.

"Would you like any help, Ma'am?" one of the missionaries asked.

"We could wash dishes or help with another chore," the other one offered.

I knew they weren't trying to pity me; they genuinely wanted to help. Since I despised washing dishes, I took them up on their offer. I spent most of my days home alone with Elizabeth, which I cherished, but I desperately missed being a part of a world where I could relay my opinions and have adult conversations. The newborn phase is beautiful, yet I needed more stimulation, which is why I was solving a Math equation before the missionaries came to the house.

"You know," Elder Ned, one of the missionaries, started to say, "I didn't always believe in religion."

Well, this is taking an interesting turn.

"What do you mean?" I inquired, sitting on a brown chair in the kitchen with Beth.

"Well, I was really hesitant that being a Mormon was something important in my life. I had friends who became so stressed out, and I started to associate stress with Mormonism," he explained. "But when I met with the Church Elders one afternoon, I was able to calmly express my frustration and hesitation, and they listened. They didn't demean me, as I thought they would. I felt heard."

I put Beth down in her bassinet – we had a few around the house for her to lay down – and took a deep breath.

"I've always wanted to feel heard." My voice was barely audible. It was more than a whisper. When you admit something that you've been thinking about for years on end, it's hard to hear yourself say those thoughts aloud.

"Well," Elder Brac, the other missionary, stated, "this is your chance, Ma'am. We're not here to push Mormonism down your throat, but we do know that this church is extremely accepting of all, no matter the viewpoints."

I began to tell them my story of growing up and attending Seventh Day Adventist Church and how I never really felt I could be myself.

Elder Ned and Elder Brac finished the dishes, tag-teaming the washing and the drying. They turned around and looked at me.

"I want to reiterate this," said Elder Ned. "We're not here to tell you how to live your life. But becoming a part of the LDS Church can help you reclaim yourself and find your purpose."

Before they left, they invited me to join them at church every Sunday. For weeks on end, I made an excuse as to why I couldn't attend. In the meantime, I eventually picked up the Book of Mormon, and I started to read a little bit at a time. After reading and praying, I woke up one morning and remembered the most magnificent dream.

I pictured myself wide awake, standing on the back verandah at my parents' home. I looked up at the clear blue sky and suddenly, out of nowhere, came this shiny, gorgeous golden chariot descending from the heavens. I felt my cheeks burning with pride and excitement as I saw Jesus coming down to Earth from the skies. When I awoke, I felt myself smiling – a smile I hadn't experienced for months. The next time Ned and Brac invited me to join them at church, I didn't make any excuses. I was ecstatic to attend for the first time.

The church was held in an old, abandoned theatre in Highgate, St. Mary. There were cracks in the board walls and the sunlight filtered through. Only about eight people were in attendance, including myself, Ned, and Brac. The service started with the sacrament meeting, then each of us had the opportunity to share our own individualized testimonies afterwards. I felt at peace while I was there. For the first time in a long time, I had an enlightening experience with religion, and I felt an urge to get baptized through this particular church. Elizabeth came with me every Sunday, and after several weeks, I decided to become an official member. My sister, Bingy, joined me, and we were both baptized at the same time. Becoming a Mormon helped fulfill a greater spiritual need that I was seeking at the time and which was missing from my life. My mother and my other sisters also joined the LDS church a few months after I joined them in California. My niece also joined, but later married a Jew and converted to Judaism.

The doctrines of the churches I went to in my childhood years were similar to the LDS Church. Being ignorant of the doctrines of the Mormon church then, my initial thought was that it was a cult, mainly because that was all hearsay. As a young child, I tended to believe what my loved ones would tell me about our own religion and other religions, until I started questioning my own faith.

I came to understand that polygamy was a practice in the early days of the LDS Church but was later abolished. There were individuals who did not agree with this change, so they broke away from LDS and reformed their own version of the Mormon Church, which included the practice of polygamy. They are two different sects to this day.

After reading more and more about LDS, I realized that the Book of Mormon spoke the truth, and Joseph Smith was, in fact, a prophet I believe ordained by God. The Oxford dictionary defines a prophet as a person regarded as an inspired teacher or a proclaimer of the will of God. For me, gaining knowledge and confirming the truth about Christ and creation has ultimately broadened my understanding of life. I do not believe in conforming to any particular system that prevents me from being myself or embracing my own individual values. Labels can sometimes be misleading and often constricting. Yet becoming a member of the LDS church allowed me, and still does, to continue being who I wanted to become without any restrictions. This felt completely freeing, unlike my experience with church as a teenager. I came to recognize that the LDS members were simply a group of like-minded individuals, meeting together through fellowship in worshipping God. We were all, and continue to become, the best versions of ourselves while living in an imperfect world as imperfect beings.

Becoming a part of the LDS Church led me to value myself, my opinions, and my spirituality, which allowed me to ask myself questions like, "Who do I want to become in life?" and "How can I achieve my goals and dreams?" and "Where is my spirituality leading me in terms of work and my personal life?"

Throughout my spiritual journey, Devon supported me. I wanted him to join me in the LDS Church, but he never considered religion to be an important part of his life as an individual. Devon did attend a Methodist Church as a child and was enrolled in a Seventh-Day Adventist school in his primary years, yet he didn't care much about religious expression.

Many years later when I moved back home to Jamaica with my children, I didn't make the time or effort to continue attending church due to work. The desire has always been there, but I had also reached a point in my life where I could pray to God and have that heavenly relationship with Him myself, without feeling guilty for not attending church on a regular basis. I was at a stage where I was refining my God-given purpose in life, and I knew this is what He intended for me.

Chapter 14

Moving to the States

Shortly after Devon and I got married – and shortly before my panic attack – my mother returned to the States for work and my two youngest sisters migrated to California to join her and attend school.

After looking through programmes for Beth and seeing how she was developing in Jamaica, I made the decision to move the two of us to North Hollywood, California to be closer to my mother and siblings. I left Jamaica for California with the intention to seek out therapy for Beth, further my education and earn enough to ensure the security of my family. Compared to Jamaica, California was a kingdom for the therapies that Beth needed to thrive. While I still love my home country, Jamaica wasn't able to offer what our family needed at the time. Daddy was still traveling back and forth, so I couldn't take into consideration his whereabouts when making this decision for my family. The fact that Mummy was also willing to help me with Beth was a huge reason for us to make the move. She supported the idea of me attending college and starting to work for myself. I was a bit hesitant at first since I knew her value system differed from mine, yet I was pleasantly surprised when she said lovingly, "Yes, go do your thing, Sandy. I will help you with Beth. Whatever you need."

At the time, Devon had no intentions of ever leaving Jamaica. He loved his work and being close to his roots so he refused to leave our homeland, though he did visit us in California frequently. We were both concerned about Elizabeth's development in Jamaica, too, and agreed that she would need more therapy than Jamaica could offer. We also agreed that while I took Elizabeth to California, I could get a work permit and save more money so we could build a house as a family. Though Devon supported this decision, it was very tough for both of us; we felt as though we were leaving a part of our hearts behind, even though we knew this was the best decision for our daughter at the time. While I would have loved to be together as a family of three, the circumstances didn't pan out that way, at least in Beth's early years.

My life's focus became securing the future of my daughter's needs and comforts. Though I recognized that she would be disabled her whole life, accepting this was a tough pill to swallow. A month after I got baptized through the LDS Church, I boarded a flight at the Sangster International Airport in Montego Bay, Jamaica to Los Angeles, California with Elizabeth in my arms. When we moved to California, I immediately felt at ease and at peace with my decision. I knew that these therapies wouldn't be able to reverse her disabilities, but I also knew she desperately needed more help than she was getting at home in Jamaica. Elizabeth was able to get all the necessary tests done at the UCLA Pediatric Genetic Center and it was finally ruled out that she did not have a chromosome abnormality. With every task – grocery shopping, applying to LA College (formerly ICT), discovering the best and brightest therapists for Beth – I would affirm that I could be as successful as anyone else. In fact, I would be even more successful, because I approached everything in my life with dedication and tenacity. My overall agenda was to succeed. I was driven and determined to live my life according to my terms, and though I was a young mother with a disabled daughter, these factors wouldn't stop me. In fact, having Elizabeth gave me a renewed sense of purpose and a new lease of life. She propelled my life forward in ways I could never have imagined prior to my life without her. Her life gave my life more purpose beyond my wildest imagination. She was never like any other child; her personality showed through her laughter and physical movements and still does to this day.

*

My mother and two youngest sisters lived in a two-bedroom apartment in North Hollywood, California and I went to stay with them. On the weekdays, my mother worked as a caregiver to two young children two hours away and she only came home on weekends. My two younger sisters were taking community college classes nearby. For the first few months, I had no job, so I had to rely on my mother to support us financially.

I started attending church at the studio city ward just around the corner from where we lived. My mother and two younger sisters joined me. A month after arriving in California, my sister Bingy and my niece Donnay, who I had left back in Jamaica, joined us. My mother and sisters were a huge support force for me and Elizabeth. When I got a job and Beth started school, everyone took turns helping out where they could.

I was visiting the US on a visitor's visa at the time. I applied for an extension, checked into the college I previously attended and applied for a student visa and work permit. Three months later, I received my temporary green card, as well as Devon's and Elizabeth's. Several more months passed, and our permanent green cards came in the mail; I was ecstatic, yet Devon didn't particularly care one way or another. He didn't ever intend on settling permanently in the United States, and I knew I wouldn't live in the US for my entire adult life.

I went to classes in the morning and went to work in the afternoons until I graduated after a year with an Associates Degree in Business Management from LA College (formerly ICT). After that, I started working during the days and attending classes in the evenings to further my education. My mother moved into a three-bedroom apartment, and I got a one-bedroom apartment two floors down from hers. I only stayed at my apartment when Devon came to visit; I figured it was an incentive for him to stay longer, yet he was rarely able to visit for more than a couple of weeks at a time, as he couldn't be away from work for that long. When Devon wasn't visiting, the routine shifted. I would stop at my mom's apartment in the evenings to pick up Beth after school. Instead of walking down two sets of stairs, I would close my eyes besides Beth. She would snuggle into the corner of my arms – a perfect fit – and we would fall asleep within minutes of each other on a small bed adjacent to my mother's bed in her room. I have always treasured those days, where we could be so close to our supportive family and know that we were always taken care of at the end of each day. I always sang to Beth – "Twinkle Star" – more for myself, but also because I knew music was soothing to her. She couldn't speak, yet her facial expressions and her eyes told a story in themselves.

*

I teamed up with my mother and sisters and purchased a large, unfinished house in Chatsworth, California. Overtime we put the finishing touches on the house and the value gradually increased. I had never particularly been handy, yet I've always enjoyed problem-solving. I took a look at the floor in my bedroom, for instance; it was a dark brown wooden floor with the grooves clearly visible and people below would hear when someone was walking above, so I decided to install cozy carpeting to soundproof the floor and make the floor more comfortable to walk on. After contemplating how to install the carpet myself, I informed my mother and sisters, and we went to work. Each project in the house was like this – painting, installing a new stovetop, the paving of our pool deck, and so much more. We sometimes woke up at 4 a.m. to work on house projects ourselves. We knew we could have hired more contractors to do the work, but there was something beautiful and magical about completing the work ourselves, especially as a group of women. This ultimately strengthened our relationships as well, and when the house projects were mostly completed – I say "mostly" because there are always projects when you own a house – we were able to relax, knowing we put this together ourselves.

When I wasn't getting dust on myself from a house project, I was in North Hollywood working at a recording studio. Clients who booked studio time would occasionally require catering, which wasn't a service the company officially offered. Since I wanted to satisfy the clients' needs, I was pushed into providing this service on an ad hoc basis, setting up the catering and charging an extra fee.

The first time I was asked to do this type of service was for a rushed casting call, which paid $1,500. The out-of-pocket cost was only $300, so I netted $1,200. When I couldn't complete the transaction myself, I hired a separate assistant to do the work and netted a bit less. The company was satisfied with how I was helping their clients, and so they let me pursue this side endeavor in addition to my monthly salary.

Looking back, this experience was truly my first act of entrepreneurship. Working at this recording studio allowed me to become a sophisticated, career-driven woman. I had a taste of what it was like to work and be in the company of talented people, including notable business executives, musicians, actors, directors, and producers. I had no intention of ever going back to my panic attack days, where I would constantly belittle myself and ask aloud, "Who am I? What am I meant to become? What should I do?"

I continued to pursue my education, as that had always been crucial to my understanding of the world. Negative thoughts were things of the past; I had no time to pursue these egregious, torturous mindset blocks that used to take up so much mental space. I drove a brand-new black Mercedes Benz and I lived in a beautiful, newly-remodeled home, had wonderful friends, and felt as though I could finally enjoy my life. I attended church each Sunday morning and kept busy throughout the week. I was finally giving myself permission to enjoy my life on my own terms, though I did miss Devon terribly when he was in Jamaica. Though I was experiencing joy in my own life, my heart suffered immensely as we couldn't spend a significant amount of time together. Devon was in charge of managing the guesthouse business a few years before my departure to the US, and it was thriving. Our collective plan was for Elizabeth to remain in the US for as long as possible in order to receive the therapy she needed, yet neither Devon nor I knew how difficult it would be to be apart for years at a time, though we knew this decision was in the best interest of our daughter.

I felt as though there were two sides of my life – one where Elizabeth was thriving, which put a smile on my face daily, and one where I longed for my family to be together as a unit. I was pulled in two directions for a number of years, yet the business of life didn't allow me to process these thoughts until much later on.

I called Devon one evening after Elizabeth was in bed, as I always did every single night, and broke down for the first time in months.

"Dev, I really miss you," I cried to him over the phone. "I love my life here, but I so wish you were a part of it on a permanent basis."

I felt silence on the other end of the call as I knew Devon was processing what I had just said.

"Sandy, this was our choice collectively… you knew it would be difficult but wanted to pursue it anyways," he casually said. "I'm proud of you for taking care of our daughter so well, and taking care of yourself, too."

"I don't know how much longer I can do this here," I whispered, the black landline shaking in my right hand.

"Hey, listen, it'll be alright," Devon sighed. "We're both so busy right now with work, and you're going to school still, too. I do appreciate everything you're doing to help Beth. She's thriving in the States, and that's what we wanted, remember?"

"Okay, yes," I agreed, wiping a tear away from my cheek. "I'll give myself and Elizabeth some more time here then."

"Goodnight, babe."

Devon hung up the phone before I could respond, yet I knew he was right. It was a simple reminder of the fact that we had a special needs child who needed proper care, and Devon and I didn't have the prerequisites to know exactly what to do to help Beth thrive. That night, I decided I would try to give Beth two more years of therapy before moving back to Jamaica. Though she wasn't speaking still, she was receiving physical, occupational, and speech therapy. When Beth turned seven years old, she finally began to walk. I couldn't have been prouder of her, and she was proud of herself, too. I was elated that she had learned to walk, and our hope as a family was for her to learn how to speak as well. While she did learn a lot in language therapy, she is still unable to speak to this day, yet her facial expressions can tell us what she's thinking.

Chapter 15

Flying Adventures

After a few years of Devon living with Beth and me on and off, we started to discuss the idea of us having some time to ourselves. Though Beth was doing well, all things considered, Devon and I both missed spending quality time with one another. Since he was a pilot and had pursued aviation in California, we found a flight charter company close to where we lived, and he would rent a plane himself, flying solo. One day, he invited me to go with him.

Perhaps this can be a fun couple's activity for us, I thought.

"What a great idea!" I exclaimed excitedly, hugging him and giving him a kiss. "I can't wait!"

The following day, we made sure Beth was all set up with childcare, and Devon drove us in our black Mercedes to the airport, which was about forty-five minutes away from where we lived in Chatsworth. The small airport was gorgeous; planes of all sizes lined up neatly and evenly across the runway.

Devon already knew the drill since he had been here before. He gave them his ID and pilot's license, then we were able to choose which plane we'd fly for a two-hour window of time. It would cost $134 per hour, at least. Devon decided we'd "wet rent" the plane, so the cost of oil and fuel would be included or reimbursed in the total charge. This was also the first time Devon had flown a plane with just the two of us. As always, I observed the others at the airbase, and I looked to glean any sort of safety information I could.

All I knew was that I trusted Devon with my whole heart, and he had enough experience to make me feel safe. I always felt safe and protected when I was with Devon.

"Don't worry," he said when he saw me observing. "The weather conditions are perfect today. Look, see? It's 80 degrees and sunny, not a cloud in the sky. The airfield conditions are superb today as well. Even the smug is minimal."

I smiled and nodded, knowing he was right. He was usually right about almost everything. Except when he wasn't.

We walked to a Cessna 172 SP and climbed in. Devon reached over, making sure my seatbelt was secure and fastened, and we put on our headsets so we could chat in the air.

"Isn't this gorgeous?" Devon smiled at me, taking my hand in his when we were up at a safe distance in the air. "I'm so happy we get to do this together, Sandy. What a beautiful day."

I squeezed his hand in return, acknowledging how much I appreciated this time with him. Time together was rare these days, as Devon only visited Beth and I every couple of months.

"This landscape is just beautiful," I told him. And it was the truth. While I had been on several planes in my life, I had never witnessed such glorious beauty from the front part of the plane. The trees and streets resembled rainbow-coloured post-it notes. Cars looked like they were straight out of Mario Kart. As the plane climbed and we approached Big Bear, the trees seemed endless, expanding for miles while the white capped mountain stared back at me majestically and Lake Tahoe sat still to one side between the California Nevada border. I couldn't help but think that this was the best it would ever be between my husband and I. This was the first of several flights and countless adventures together.

Chapter 16

A Relocation

Since Elizabeth was making so much progress in the United States, I did not want to uproot her. Yet I knew if I could relocate to Florida, which was significantly closer to Jamaica, I might be happier, and our family would be able to visit one another more regularly. I went online and researched schools and houses in Florida. After putting the Chatsworth house on the market in California, I found a house in the Orlando area. I immediately put a deposit on the house and applied for a home loan. We relocated to Florida in a matter of weeks, and I resigned from my job at the recording studio. I had learned so much there, but it was time for a change of scenery.

By this time, my two younger sisters had moved out and were married; while we remained close, they wanted to pursue lives of their own. My mother, my sister Bingy, and my niece moved with me and Beth to Florida. Beth was able to attend a new school with a fantastic special ed program.

It took the Chatsworth house three months to sell, but then reality hit me when I looked at my bank account. I had a tidy sum of cash in there, and Devon and I were elated at the amount of savings we had accumulated over the years, combined with the gains from the sale of the house. We had spent so much money, time, and energy on two separate living arrangements and Beth's medical needs, we had moved past the days when we were counting pennies in order to figure out how we'd make our money work together for the following month's expenses. It was a huge relief to get to this point in our lives.

When I knew Beth was happy in school and benefiting from the therapies she needed, it was time for me to decide what to do career-wise in Florida. I knew I wanted to try something different than being at a recording studio. Besides, California had a plethora of those, yet Florida wasn't necessarily known for having famous clients walking into music or movie productions.

I had experience working in the printing industry several years prior, and so I pursued the idea of becoming a print franchisee. I figured I could set up the business easily and leave for Jamaica when my homesickness inevitably became worse. After finding a print franchise, I formed my own LLC and signed a franchise agreement in Orlando. The franchise headquarters was based in Salt Lake City, Utah, and so I flew there for a few days to get trained; Beth stayed with my mom in Florida. When I came back home, I began prospecting and looking for a location to set up my new franchise. One of the prospects I visited was quite memorable. He was a chiropractor who studied ancient Chinese medicine. Out of the blue, he asked me, "So how far along are you?" I was completely shocked and appalled. Devon and I hadn't necessarily been trying to have another baby. It was something we had discussed at one point, but with Beth's multitude of needs, we just never got around to it, though I was thinking more frequently about having another child.

"You're two months pregnant," the chiropractor told me, staring into my eyes unblinkingly. He grabbed hold of my wrists tightly and added, "Would you like to know the gender of your baby?"

My mind was spinning a million miles a minute. Two seconds ago, I didn't know I was pregnant. Now, I had not only heard that I was pregnant, but I was also going to find out the gender of my second baby. I was flabbergasted, but in a good way. The best way.

"Yes," I whispered softly as he continued to hold my wrists in place.

The chiropractor maneuvered my hands around in a circular motion, and he closed his eyes, humming and meditating to himself.

"I'm feeling male energy," he informed me. He opened his eyes once again. "You're having a boy."

I left his office feeling queasy. My heartburn had been worse the past few weeks, but I had attributed it to flying and running around, trying to get the franchise off the ground, take care of the new house, Beth, my mom, and myself. Now I knew I was mistaken. There was a new life forming inside of me. I smiled to myself, and I couldn't wait to tell Devon this exciting news.

I had grand plans to prospect for several months before buying a franchise location, and I felt excited at the notion of owning a business for the very first time. I had slightly dipped my toes in the entrepreneurship world during my time at the recording studio, yet this felt significantly different.

After a number of weeks went by, my pregnancy became more burdensome. It was more difficult to walk around and continue prospecting, and I continuously felt ill. I would bring water with me everywhere, yet I felt like I could never completely quench my thirst. I spoke with the head office of the franchise, and ultimately, we decided collectively that I should wait to pursue this endeavor further until after my baby boy arrived. I was disappointed and relieved simultaneously; I had been so thrilled to start this franchise, yet at the same time, I knew I had to take care of my body and my son in utero.

When I told Devon the news, he began discussing how I could still earn an income during my pregnancy. Since relocating to Florida, we had become friendly with the owner of a flight school and charter company nearby. During one of our many dates there, we ran into him and told him about our dilemma. He informed us that we could become aircraft owners and have the aircraft managed by the charter company. Devon and I immediately purchased a Cessna 172 airplane, which started earning income right away. Within a month, we knew that this income would take care of my monthly living expenses as well as the monthly payments for the aircraft.

The charter company maintained custody of the aircraft and charged a 20% maintenance fee on charters. If we needed to use the aircraft, we would have to book it for the time slot. It was always fully booked, so we usually had to book another one. I remember one time when we flew to visit my mom in Marathon where she was working. Devon's mother was visiting us, so Devon rented a plane and flew us over to Marathon so we could all meet up and have lunch with my mom.

My pregnancy chugged along, and I became more and more reserved. Though I had found a spark within myself when living in California, I felt that spark dissipate as time went on in Florida, and I saw my husband less and less. It's a strange feeling being pregnant, living with your mother and daughter, but knowing that your husband is an ocean away. Yet I didn't want to allow these negative emotions to overtake me once again, like they had when Elizabeth was a baby. I was determined to learn more about myself and what I was capable of, and part of this was understanding what kind of mother I knew I could be to my unborn son. I prayed each Sunday at church for a healthy baby boy. Churchgoers and community members in Orlando frequently came up to me and patted my belly with smiles and expectant glances.

"Oh! You're having a boy, how perfect! One girl, one boy. Just perfect!" they'd exclaim.

But what if I was having another girl? Would she not be as important, simply because she wouldn't be a boy? These thoughts stirred my mind into the night, and it was getting more difficult to become well-rested as my belly grew bigger and bigger.

*

When I was thirty-nine weeks pregnant, I was driving my SUV on a wet road after picking up my sister from the airport. The speedometer read 5 mph, as I was in congested traffic. Suddenly, a car came up behind me going at least 20 mph and collided into my SUV. I felt my neck sway back and forth and utter shock flooded my mind.

Would I be okay?

What would Beth do without me?

Is my baby boy okay?!

The paramedics arrived minutes later after the driver of another car had called. I was transported to the hospital minutes later, only taking my purse while my sister followed in the SUV. I was feeling a bit woozy but okay overall, yet the nurses and doctors insisted on checking on the baby. They took scans and measured my belly. The ultrasound was perfect. I called my mother to ensure Beth would be cared for that evening; my mother was incredibly concerned about the baby, as was Devon.

I was kept overnight with a band across my stomach to see if I was having any contractions, which, thankfully, I was not. I didn't want my son to come into the world before he was ready to do so, and I certainly was concerned that a car accident would induce labor. The next morning, I called Devon and my mother back-to-back, letting them know I would be released from the hospital, and I then made the necessary arrangements to have my sister collect me from the hospital. The doctors and nurses were thankful that all my tests looked completely normal. We all prayed to God for the blessings we received within those twenty-four hours. A car crash is an extremely alarming experience, but when you are pregnant, such an incident is three times scarier. This experience made me realize that as much as I wanted the best for Beth, I also needed my family to be whole – I wanted what was best for me as well as my family, and that was for us to be together. So, I started to plan my move back to Jamaica after the baby was born, even though Devon insisted that I wait until after the house in Jamaica was more livable.

Several days later, I went into labor early in the morning. The contractions were getting more intense at a quicker pace than last time. I called Devon and he flew from Jamaica to Orlando, arriving home that evening. We went to the hospital, placing Beth in the care of my mother, and we checked into the Labor & Delivery unit. My doctor was on vacation, and he was not expected back for another two weeks. The nurse practitioner from my doctor's office came and advised that the doctor on duty would attend to me, which was such a blessing. After I tried pushing for more than two hours, the doctor looked at me, then Devon, and said very calmly, "We're going to have to do an emergency C-section. Baby's heart rate is dropping." I looked at Devon and we both nodded.

I was wheeled to the operating room. At this point, it was 5 a.m. the following morning. I already had an epidural, and while it was an emergency C-section, I didn't need general anesthesia. A half hour later, I met my beautiful baby boy, who was perfect in every way. He had ten fingers, ten toes, and a strong cry. I named him Milan, and fell in love all over again. Before having him, I wasn't sure how I could love someone as much as I already loved Elizabeth. But now I knew that my capacity to love was larger than I had ever realized. Though Elizabeth still couldn't speak, her eyes lit up, and her face exhibited a radiant smile when I brought Milan home for the first time.

Chapter 17

The Arrest

Life threw me a huge, personal curveball just over a week after Milan was born via an emergency C-section.

A California lawyer who I was acquainted with, named Cornell, called me one day to inform me of some disturbing news.

"Sandy, I have some terrible news, and I know you just had a baby, but this couldn't wait," Cornell said as he sighed over the phone. I had no idea what could be so urgent that he couldn't have waited a few weeks to tell me.

"A grand jury just met in Kansas, and your name was somehow brought up in an indictment," he said with hesitation in his voice. "They're saying you were a part of an elaborate conspiracy … I don't know any more details than that, but I saw your name pop up on a legal blog, and I knew I had to call you."

I laughed, which immediately hurt. Having a C-section also means having no abdominal strength, and so anytime I sat up or laughed, I would cry out, "Ouch!" simultaneously.

"Is this a joke, Cornell? Are you playing a trick on me? I've *never* been involved in any type of illegal activity in my life."

"I promise you, I'm not. I wish I was, trust me," he said. "If I were you, I would engage an attorney immediately and report to the Sheriff's office."

Part of me thought this was some large, disgusting prank. But another part of me was extremely scared.

What the hell could this be about?

Before getting off the phone, Cornell gave me the contact for a lawyer he recommended in Florida to represent me. When I called him, he said he'd meet with me the very next day; Milan would be eleven days old by then.

But it was too late.

By the time I sat down to process this horrific, strange news, the US Marshals arrived at my house in Orlando. My family had no idea what was happening. The marshals were kind to me as I invited them inside our home. They showed me a variety of photos, asking me if I recognized anyone.

"Her," I pointed. "I saw her once while living in California ages ago. It was at some music-related event, as I worked at a recording studio back then. She was related to a relative of mine. The only communication we had at this event was a brief hello. She somehow got my number sometime after, and she called me for the first time ever and was extremely unkind and strange towards me. She even accused me of writing an incriminating letter about her, and said if she went down, she would take me down with her. I assured her she was mistaken. I had no idea, and still don't know, what she was referring to, so I noted her as a bit of an off-her-rocker gal and moved on with my life. I actually hung up the phone on her, which I've only done a handful of times in my life."

The US Marshals all looked at one another and told me to go with them. It seemed as though this same lady convinced an entire grand jury that I was a part of the same elaborate conspiracy that she was a part of. And to this day, I still don't even know what the conspiracy was about, and I chose not to spend any of my time trying to find out.

I stood up straight. I needed to be fearless in this moment for my family and my children, especially my baby boy. The sadness I felt leaving him at eleven days old cannot be described in words.

"Please don't worry about me, please just take care of the babies," I told Devon, my sister, and my mother. I was breastfeeding Milan, however I was also giving him formula as a backup, and so they were able to bottle feed him. Yet I knew Milan still needed his mother, and I needed him. But I couldn't think about that right now. I needed to think about what would happen the very next moment.

Once I sat down in their pickup truck, the Marshalls cuffed me, and my rights were read to me. Two Marshalls sat on either side of me while I was driven to the federal building in downtown Orlando.

How the hell could someone incriminate me without tangible evidence?

The next few days were a complete blur.

I spent hours locked in a cell, questioned, then led to a courtroom with cuffs circulating my wrists and ankles while wearing oversized, brown jail slippers. I pleaded "not guilty." The lawyer recommended to me was present for the bail hearing, and we hired him to represent me.

The prosecutor read a list of accusations that she presented to the judge, but the judge was fuming. She could see right through the prosecutor's false accusations. I couldn't be formally charged anyways, because the court was still waiting on a few documents from Kansas. The judge ruled that as soon as the documents arrived, I should be booked then granted unsecured bail.

"Continue with your education, and please take care of your family," she said. "Go home to your baby boy."

I was transported by a paneled van to a county jail to be detained until I could be formally charged. Upon arriving at the detention centre, I was to hand over any personal items I had on me, including the jewelry I was wearing. I was photographed, then escorted to a room where they tested me for TB before being taken to a holding area. The women in the small room surrounded me; the room, about 10-feet by 16-feet, had an open toilet in one corner and a pay phone adjacent to it. The temperature was around 35 degrees Fahrenheit, and my teeth were chattering. The heating was either malfunctioning, or the people in charge didn't care enough about the women here to turn it on.

"Hey girl, I'm Dana. What are you in for?"

The woman who spoke to me had long, blond hair and blue eyes. She searched my wrist tag and gave me a once-over glance.

"I was accused of conspiracy," I said shyly, not certain how these three women would react.

"Oh girl, that's nothing," said Dana.

Just then, dinner was served. Plates of meatloaf, string beans, potato, and cornbread were served. I was starving and would've eaten anything, but the first bite of meatloaf left a disgusting taste in my mouth. I hadn't truly acknowledged that I was in a jail cell until then. Eating "prison food" gave me a reality check, and I longed to hold Milan in my arms.

Dana finished her plate and started on mine.

"I'm a single mom, and I'd just lost my job," she said in between tasteless bites. "I have two kiddos in elementary school, and they were starving. I tried so hard to get the basic necessities for them without stealing, I really did. But I thought to myself, 'They deserve more than this. They deserve a Goddamn steak.' And so, I tried to steal a steak from the grocery store. But the alarm beeped, and I was caught. It really wasn't the smartest thing I could've done, but in that split second, all I wanted was for my children to not be hungry for one more damn night. They're with my parents now, and I don't know when I'll see them again. At least this time it's a misdemeanor. I gotta be smarter."

I listened intently, reminding myself that I was lucky to have my support system. Although this arrest was a horrible, torturous experience, I realized that I had Devon, my mother, my siblings, and friends who I could rely on when things got tough.

The other women proceeded to tell me their stories as well. They were both charged with misdemeanors – one for marijuana possession of fifteen grams, and another for child endangerment. A neighbour had called the police on this woman for leaving her baby in a hot car, even though the windows were rolled down. Apparently, it was 90 degrees Fahrenheit that day, and the neighbour was concerned. My cellmate claimed she was running into her apartment to get the diaper bag, since she forgot it, and she didn't think it would be a "big deal" to leave her newborn alone for just a few minutes. But she was wrong, and now she wasn't with her newborn. She was eating string beans with a bunch of strange women, including myself.

I pinched myself and shook my head. Perhaps if I had red shoes, I could've tapped my heels together three times, crossed my fingers, and said, "There's no place like home. There's no place like home. There's no place like home." The reality was that I was stuck in a US jail overnight. I remembered the pay phone and walked over to use it. I was allowed a five-minute phone call, and so I called home to check on my babies.

"Mummy? Mummy, it's me. It's Sandy," I said with desperation. "How are they? How are they doing? I can't believe I've been away from Milan for a full day already. I miss him terribly. Beth, too. And you, and Devon, and everyone else."

I wore a brave face, as per usual, and didn't let tears fall, mainly because I knew my mom would be even more upset if she knew how terrible I felt.

"They're okay," Mummy said, her voice shaky. Hearing the sadness and worry in my mother's voice made my knees buckle in plain sight.

"How are you holding up?"

"Oh, I'm fine, Mummy," I said, continuing to hold back tears. Of course, I wasn't fine. Who is fine in a jail cell?! But she needed to know that I was fine, and so that's what I said.

"It's a huge misunderstanding, Mummy, I'll be home tomorrow."

"Okay Sandy. We told Beth you said happy birthday. She looked confused but tried to understand."

"Okay, thank you."

I had missed Elizabeth's eighth birthday – I had never once missed her birthday, and to this day, that's the only birthday celebration of hers I've ever missed. While Elizabeth couldn't talk yet, she knew it was her birthday, and she loved celebrating in style. We usually bought a chocolate cake, her favourite, and decorated it ourselves with an exorbitant amount of frosting in all different colors, especially purple. She loved the color purple.

I wondered if Devon knew where to get her chocolate cake. Did they buy a chocolate cake for her? Maybe my mother knew. I should've told Mummy that the frosting and cake decorating tools were in the cupboard to the left of the sink. I wasn't sure about much anymore, but right then, all I could think about was Elizabeth's confusion about why her Mama wasn't home to celebrate her birthday.

I tried to fall asleep in the plastic tub with the thin sheet pressed above my chin. Tears finally allowed themselves to sprinkle across my face. At night, jails are one of the saddest places on earth. Whimpering comes from all over, every corner of the place. I felt sad knowing not only my own situation, but those of the women I shared a cell with, too. How many others here were trying to live their daily lives, watching their kids starve, and attempting to do whatever they could to survive?

The next morning, a guard called my name, and I stood up straight. My back was sore from the plastic bed and thin mattress, and it took my body awhile to walk properly again, especially since I was still recovering from my C-section. My personal items were returned to me, and I stepped through a door and into freedom. I had never been so happy to breathe fresh air. I spotted Devon waiting for me and seeing him gave me renewed strength as we embraced. He drove us home to our babies. Before I held Milan, I took a steaming hot two-minute shower, which was the best shower of my entire life.

The following day, I did a pre-trial check-in. After starting up a conversation with the pre-trial clerk, he explained in detail what was going to happen.

"Wait, but how can someone be arrested for something they didn't do without any existing proof?"

He chuckled.

"Unfortunately, this is a common occurrence," he said in a hushed tone. "This is just the US Justice system for you. Anyone can get arrested by simply knowing someone who committed the crime… and hey, you'll also have to fly to Kansas to attend your court hearing."

I stumbled for a moment, even more confused than I was a few minutes ago.

"Wait, what? At my own expense?"

He nodded.

"I've never heard of something that ridiculous."

Although I would have been able to use a federal public defender, I spoke to a different attorney who told me what it would cost to hire him to represent me, as if I had really committed a crime. It would cost me thousands upon thousands of dollars, more than every penny Devon and I had combined.

Immediately after this conversation, I went home and wrote letters to all my creditors letting them know I would be unable to continue paying my mortgage and my car expenses.

At that point, I had decided what was best for my family – I was going to move back to Jamaica. I could no longer be in the States with this trial hanging over my head.

Against legal advice, I wrote a letter to the judge, thanking her and apologizing to her. In the letter, I told her that I shouldn't be put through such an unfair system which would cost me everything I had, waste my time, and waste the court's time when I knew I did nothing wrong, and had faith that the truth will come to light. In addition, I couldn't bear the thought of being away from my children again for a split second. Being away from Milan for a whole day and night was already too much, since he was a tiny newborn who needed me, and I was still recovering from surgery. I felt the need to explain my personal choice to her, because I didn't want to come across as having any disrespect towards her or the court system. Though I, once again, tried to be brave, I was under so much pressure and chose my children, even if this meant I could never step foot in the States again. Nothing mattered more than my family.

The California lawyer I knew called me the following week to ask why I didn't show up for court.

"I'm not in the country, and I don't plan to return until my name is cleared," I told him. "I don't have any intention of spending my savings on something this trivial and comical."

Weeks later, I was officially on the most-wanted list in the States. Devon jokingly started calling me "Al Capone."

Luckily, the US charges were eventually dropped, as the investigators couldn't find any evidence to continue a case against me. Yet this was still an extremely traumatic experience, and I felt the need to completely start anew. I firmly believed in the idea of giving up some luxuries in order to get a fresh start at home in Jamaica, and so that's what we did. Cleansing myself of the trauma took many years, yet I was still able to forgive the culprits who put me in this predicament to begin with.

Years later, I decided to venture back to the US with Devon, just the two of us. When I arrived at immigration, the officer asked me if I was ever arrested.

"Yes," I told him truthfully, "but the charges were dropped."

It took less than an hour, but after he looked up my file, he cleared me to enter the US. As soon as he did, I felt a huge weight lifted off of my shoulders. Devon smiled at me, knowing how important this was. The whole ordeal was finally over, and I could travel back and forth between the US and Jamaica whenever I pleased.

Chapter 18

Home-Bound

The added stress of the arrest and charges, as well as my postpartum struggles, threatened to drive me into a state of depression. I knew the move back to Jamaica may negatively affect Elizabeth's progress at this point, and I knew I would need to homeschool her, but my mental health was in serious decline. We needed to be back home.

My mom stayed in Orlando for a brief period of time but then moved back as well to join us and my other siblings who still resided in Jamaica at the time. For weeks, I had slowly packed up while in the early stages of postpartum, whilst caring for Elizabeth simultaneously. I was still feeling a little weak, however I decided to fly, nonetheless. My emotional state was in overdrive, and I felt it was time to go home.

I resigned myself to the fact that my husband needed to be a constant presence in our children's life and my life. I ended up having to take an earlier flight, while Devon and the children took a later flight. It was quite heroic of Devon to take on the responsibility to fly with them both all by himself, but he managed. It was no easy feat, flying with my eight-year-old special needs child and a newborn, but we accomplished it thanks to Devon. I made sure to keep all records of Elizabeth's schooling as well as Milan's pediatric reports. I prayed for adequate weather and no flight delays. When they landed at Norman Manley International Airport in Kingston, Jamaica, several hours after me, I greeted them with hugs and kisses. My mother and my sister completed my packing and shipped off my things to me, so I did not have to take a trip back as initially planned, as I needed time to get situated.

Devon placed Milan in his car seat and strapped him in and then he did the same with Beth like the pro-dad he was, and we drove to our home in Portland, which was still under construction with only one room and one bathroom that were fully functioning. The rest of the house had no flooring or doors; it was an adventure, to say the least. Tiling the floors happened next, and my brother-in-law assisted my husband in building a kitchen table so we would have a place to eat. They made a brown, wooden table that sat up to eight individuals at a time; they used their creative genius to build the most gorgeous rustic table I had ever seen. Though it was originally meant to be a kitchen table, it was our multi-functioning house table. I used it as my desk, the dining room table, the kitchen table, the countertop, and even Milan's play area. I would spoon feed both Milan and Elizabeth while using my laptop on that table. One afternoon, I turned my back to Milan for half a second to get a spoon, and he decided to pick out the keys on the keyboard. He did this twice, both times choosing "F" and the "Alt" keys. I laughed the first time until I realized the cost of replacing the keyboard; the second time wasn't as funny, but again, he was a baby, and he was playing. He didn't know any better. I tried hard to contain and control any anger I felt so I didn't appear angry with my children. I didn't want my kids to grow up in a house full of anger and resentment, and so I did my best to hide my feelings and put on a smile for their sake every single day. It was difficult, though, as a stay-at-home mom in those days. Because our location in Jamaica didn't have the proper programming for Beth at the time, I homeschooled her. We did stimulatory exercises, practiced holding objects, feeding herself, and walking up and down the staircase. Books were a huge part of her development and growth as well. My schedule looked something like this:

1. Get up, one hour on the treadmill.
2. Make breakfast.
3. Feed my children.
4. Give them their baths.
5. Put them on a rug in the living room to play.
6. Clean up the kitchen and the rest of the house.
7. Prepare lunch and dinner.
8. Read to the kids before bedtime.
9. Shower after the kids go to bed.
10. Study/research on my laptop.

I was still in education mode, in the midst of completing yet another degree; I was forever a student. I would get up early each morning to do a walk/run combination on the treadmill, which was in the living room. I had borrowed this particular treadmill from my parents' house, who told me to just keep it since it wasn't getting used at their house. The goal was to eventually have a recreational space, and we'd move the treadmill there eventually. Looking back, I realize that having this time to myself in the morning really nourished my soul. I felt as though I was constantly cleaning, cooking, and doing something for someone else each minute of the day. But these minutes in the morning were my own time, and the exercise also helped my body get back into shape after Milan's birth.

While I was still an extremely reserved and introverted person, I still longed for adult conversation. This time in my life was similar to when the Mormon missionaries visited me, witnessing Elizabeth as a newborn. Elizabeth's early years were so similar to Milan's in terms of how I took care of myself; adult conversations were very few and far between. Though I did see Devon at night, he felt the opposite of me; he was tired of talking to adults all day and wanted to sleep. Devon's uncle owned a home in Spring Garden, a gorgeous area just outside of Buff Bay in Portland. I would strap both children into their car seats and head there some evenings, which was my only source of socialization outside of the house. I would unbuckle them both and carry them to my uncle's house, holding one on each side. To me, it was worth the effort of driving ten minutes each way in order to see family and have those adult conversations that I so craved back in those days.

*

Cleaning the house began to drain me inside and out. Though the house was still fairly empty and void of furniture, I still felt the impulse to clean every single day. Taking care of my children and the house were exhausting, and by the end of the day, I rarely found time or energy to leave the house and do something for myself, whether it was meeting up with a friend or going over to my parents' house for dinner. At the time, Devon's heavy equipment business was thriving, and we had some extra money to hire help. Together, Devon and I decided it would be beneficial for me – both mentally and physically – to have someone around the house to clean and help me take care of our children.

The idea was grander than the execution, though. We went through a half dozen interviews at least, and we hired a few different individuals over a period of several weeks. One woman approached my house, introduced herself, and while walking into my home, she informed me that she was a diabetic and could only eat wholewheat; she asked me for a snack before I had asked her any questions. I sighed and attempted to continue the interview, outlining what needed to get done on a daily basis. She barely assisted Elizabeth that first morning, and then she proceeded to sit by the table and waited on me to feed her lunch. She anticipated and expected her meal to be ready for her promptly at noon, even though that was when Elizabeth needed to be eating. I smiled politely, took cash out of my wallet, and handed it to her.

"This arrangement is not working, please do not return," I told her kindly yet strongly. She looked a bit shocked and confused, and I led her to the door. When you open the door for someone to leave your house, it's a distinct clue that the guest is no longer welcome, and they have stayed past their welcome. It did take her a bit of time to "find her shoes" as she tried to sneak another piece of wholewheat bread from the kitchen.

Another promising lady told me that she had five children of her own, and I was grateful to hear that, I assumed she understood, being a mother herself. She lived up the road just walking distance from my home which made it seem even more promising. The interview had gone well, and I had an errand to run on her first day. I was only gone for about an hour, but when I came home, my house was destroyed. The woman's five children were present and running around and through the house. Breadcrumbs covered the floor. The once immaculate table – our only table still – was completely covered with dirty tissues, half-eaten sandwich biscuits, and sticky wrappers, while the lady sat by the table doing nothing in particular. The worst part was finding Milan and Elizabeth in the middle of the floor crying. Milan had a dirty diaper which had never been changed, and their clothes had dark stains that weren't there before I had left. I was absolutely appalled and told the woman to take her children and leave my house at once. I didn't bother paying her, and she never asked for payment.

Weeks passed by, and I became more and more frustrated. Finding someone to help me became like another job, which I had not anticipated. When Dorrette came into our lives, though, everything changed for the better. She radiated warm, positive energy when she entered my home, and from the first time she met Elizabeth and Milan, I could tell she loved them. In fact, she loved *all* children and told me so. Beth warmed up to her incredibly quickly as well; quicker than she had even warmed up to some relatives. Dorrette's main fault was her timeliness. Due to personal circumstances, she later told me, it was difficult for her to always be on time. There were even a couple of times where she didn't call, and she didn't show up all day. Later, she apologized and promised she would be more reliable very soon. And she didn't break her promise. To this day, Dorrette still works for me and has a wonderful, endearing relationship, particularly with Beth. She went from being the most unreliable person in my life to becoming the most reliable person, as I can call on her at any hour, any day and she will present herself.

Dorrette's help allowed me to focus on my online studies as well as what type of business I wanted to pursue in Jamaica. I had known the entrepreneurial spirit was beaming inside of me, yet I wanted to look into where I could truly be successful in Jamaica's marketplace. After Dorrette left for the day, my daughter would sit next to me and watch with keen, curious eyes to see what appeared on my computer screen, and my son would crawl on top of the table and all over me, making Beth and I smile and giggle. I did attempt to ensure, however, that Milan wouldn't have access to my keyboard since I knew how much he loved to pick at the letters and numbers.

At this time, I now had a completed kitchen and a small office, consisting of a bookshelf, two small desks, and a meager filing cabinet. I had lived in a house going through renovations previously, but it was nothing compared to this. Construction workers would come in and out on a regular basis, interrupting and interacting with my family. I felt like Dorrette had become a secondary parent, helping me so much with Beth so I could focus on work. Devon left the house very early, sometimes at 5 a.m., and came home late in the evenings, occasionally as late as 1 a.m. Sleep was trivial compared to work for him. If he was working, he felt important. But this also meant he rarely spent any time with me, Beth, or Milan, and I felt neglected as a wife. Not only was he part owner in an income-generating guesthouse, which operated under the hospitality sector, he was also in the construction and heavy equipment business. He needed to make important decisions regarding heavy equipment he owned and operated as well, which kept his patience level to a bare minimum and his stress level was maxed out. Though I felt lonely, as I did in the US, I preoccupied myself with research and learning opportunities, as I always had. We were back to our normal rhythms as a married couple, though looking back, it may not have been the healthiest way of maintaining our relationship with young children.

About six months after I moved back to Jamaica, I found out that Devon was having an affair with someone else. It turned out that he had more of a separate life than I had initially realized. The affair had gone on for almost six years, and the woman lived walking distance from our house. Feelings of devastation and confusion racked my mind as I pondered how we'd make it through. Beth was almost nine years old, and Milan wasn't even a year old yet. Like the period after the molestation that I experienced as a young child, I lost my sense of self again. Any self-esteem I had built up over the years had disappeared in a heartbeat. This betrayal drove me to a state of depression, where I constantly questioned my own existence, my purpose, and what was wrong with me.

What do I deserve in life? I thought to myself the morning after I found out this news. I had stayed up crying all night long, and I couldn't even bring myself to look in the mirror. I knew my eyes would be bloodshot, and that my cheeks were red and swollen; I looked like a complete wreck to the point of no return. Continuous, confusing thoughts raced through my mind. I felt trapped in my marriage; I had invested my entire life to developing and strengthening mine and Devon's relationship, and we had young children together. I woke up crying and fighting with him, trying to have an ounce of understanding.

What did I do wrong? I wanted to know so badly. *Were you not satisfied with me?*

I asked these questions but never truly received answers. I don't know if I really wanted these answers from Devon, though; I needed to find the answers to these questions on my own, and for myself.

Words continued to sting and hurt our relationship further. The more words we spoke, the angrier both of us became. Words were a battleground between us where no one ended up winning; it was a lose-lose battle. Communication is key to a successful relationship and partnership, yet because we had spent so much time apart, it seemed we had lost our ability to communicate effectively, properly, and productively. Once again, I felt I was being pulled in two separate directions – a part of me wanted to leave and explore life on my own terms completely, and another part of me desperately wanted to stay since we did still love each other and had two children together.

One morning when Dorrette was helping with the children, I drove to see my mother, who had recently returned to Jamaica. I had told her about the betrayal, and while she was also shocked and hurt, she felt I should stay.

"You have young children, Sandy," she started to say, patting my arm, and grasping my left hand. "It must be difficult. I haven't been in your situation. Well, no one has, because no two people have the same relationship, but I still think you should try to work things out with your husband. You both still love each other, yes?"

I nodded, trying not to cry. But my lips turned upside down into a frown, and tears ran down my cheeks.

"Oh Sandy, don't cry, daughter, it'll be okay either way," she said in her comforting, soothing voice.

I nodded again, looking up at her. I wasn't sure whether or not to believe what she said, although I always knew she had the best intentions for me and the highest regard for Devon. At least she had, before this incident.

"How could he be so reckless with our marriage?" I asked her quietly, so faintly that the words barely breathed.

"I honestly don't know, my dear," my mother said. She always had an answer for everything, but right now, she had no answers, only love and empathy. "But what I do know is that you will be okay. You are a smart young lady who has a huge future ahead of you. You're not even thirty years old, Sandy. Think about what you could make in your lifetime. Think about what you could contribute. Try to think more about your positive possibilities."

I took a deep breath and sighed, exhaling all of the exhaustion, the recklessness, the horrendous feelings I now had about myself, and so much more.

When I went home that afternoon, I waited anxiously for Devon to appear, which took hours. I asked him why he felt the need to betray me. He tried to explain why he did what he did – a justification of sorts and somewhat of an apology. I tried to understand his perspective, yet I couldn't bring myself to truly understand why anyone would cheat on their spouse. After we stayed up talking, we both went to bed a bit less angry than the day before. Upon waking up in the morning, I made a huge decision – I would focus on myself and my own career goals. I reinvested in myself all over again, gradually regaining my self-confidence. I focused on the vision for not only my future, but also for my son's future and my daughter's future. Instead of directing my anger towards Devon, I turned that negative energy into positive, delightful energy for myself and what I wanted to accomplish in my life. The experience of heartbreak and betrayal taught me to recognize that when individuals are dealing with their own trauma, they may act out in different ways. They may avoid confrontation and cause harm to others in their lives. I'm a true believer in giving a loud, echoing voice to our own traumatic experiences. In order to move forward into our future, we must confront our past; otherwise, the cycle of heartbreak may continue.

The pain and memory of this incident never left me, and it still sometimes creeps up in my conscious mind now and again. Yet this incident also propelled me into becoming the woman who I am today – a strong, driven, competitive, and loving woman. Weeks later, I made the difficult decision to stay with my husband and work on our relationship. Our vows said, "For better or for worse," and this had to be the worst.

Part 3:
The Journey of Lifespan

Chapter 19

A Business Idea

The door of my office creaked open one evening while I was furiously typing away at a business plan I was devising. I had told no one about this plan yet; it was for myself.

"Sandy, I'm going to be straight with you here," said Devon, walking closer to where I sat. He hovered over me as his strong hands held the ends of the desk. I looked up at him, wondering what he had to say so desperately.

He slammed his hands onto the desk as his voice rose an octave.

"What do you intend to do with your life?" He was trying hard to not sound angry, yet his voice couldn't hide his disgust.

"You sit here for hours on end, typing away on your laptop. You never tell me or anyone else what the hell you're doing, while Dorrette takes care of the kids. Why are we even still paying her, Sandy? Tell me what you're doing with your life and your career. What is it that you want to be doing?"

I took a deep breath and tried to understand where he was coming from. After all, I didn't really have anything to hide, but no one had ever asked me what I did in my office when Dorrette was with the kids. I welcomed the attention I was receiving at the time, since Devon worked so often still and barely paid any attention to my comings and goings.

"Well, Devon … I have been working on a business plan, and I would like to share it with you. Would you like that?"

He nodded. "Go on." He motioned his two hands forward towards me, indicating that he was ready to listen. He crossed his arms and continued to stand, since there was only one chair in my office, and I was sitting on it.

"I've identified a consumer need," I began to explain. "Being an avid consumer of bottled water, I was disappointed when I came back to Jamaica from a first world country, and found that the market didn't have as many options as I felt it should. I care about satisfying my community and consumers within the community, and this has driven me to want to create a product and a brand that would enhance the lives of others through consuming healthy water, creating jobs, and activating commerce on a larger scale in the general community. This would also, ideally, raise the standard of living for many, including us, Devon."

He was listening intently. I had never seen him stare at me in that way before. For a moment, it seemed like we were partners again. The respect he had in his eyes for me was prominent, and I could feel a sense of love and warmness emanating from a few feet away.

I reminded him that I had previously worked in a variety of industries. At the time, I didn't even know if he knew all of the jobs I had taken in my life: farming scotch bonnet peppers, bookkeeping, graphic design, printing, fashion modeling, finance, the entertainment industry, marketing/sales, and administration.

"The recording studio in North Hollywood allowed me to get a small taste of what it would be like to develop, market, and sell a product," I told Devon. "I don't know if we ever had that discussion. I don't remember talking with you about that job, but I loved it so much and learned a great deal from it."

Again, Devon remained silent. He almost always had something to say, but in this case, I truly believe he wanted to listen. It was the kindest way of showing me respect for what I was sharing with him.

"Here's my budget, which includes a summary of our savings." Devon walked over to my side of the desk, and I showed him an intricate Excel spreadsheet while pointing to a few items on the list. "This is what we could sell combined with our savings to raise the initial capital."

I moved my cursor to the next sheet, which detailed the business plan.

"The operations, marketing/sales, and financial projections are all here for the first five years, Devon… I really believe in this plan and believe in myself. Are you with me?"

Devon stared at the spreadsheet for a few more minutes, contemplating what I had said. I had a difficult time reading him, and a part of me was so scared that he'd start to berate me; telling me how the plan would fail immediately, and how this was an insane idea.

But he didn't do any of that.

Instead, he turned his head to face me directly and touched his forehead to my own. Smiling, he raised his hand and delicately brushed my hair behind my ears as he whispered, "You are brilliant. This is our future together. I can see it now. You'll break down barriers and become the face of this empire. I always knew you were a star."

He kissed me passionately – a kiss that I forgot I had longed for. This kiss represented our future together, how we would work together to make our dreams – and my business plan – a reality.

I knew this plan would work; I was so confident and saw no other choice. Although Devon had an entrepreneurial spirit as well, neither of us were confident that the heavy equipment business he had started would be sustainable in the long-term. We needed financial security for our family, particularly for Beth's needs. Not only would my family be empowered financially, but society would also benefit, bringing me great joy and fulfillment. Starting this company was also a way to create jobs for youths in our neighbourhood, as there weren't many new start-ups or other entrepreneurs in the parish of Portland at the time.

Personally, I also recognized that by starting this company, Devon would help me, and it would be a project we could take on together as a power couple. Since we were still working through his betrayal, I desperately wanted him to recognize my brilliance and my overall value as a human being, not just as a wife and as a mother. Although I didn't realize it at the time, I felt I needed to prove my worth to him. If I had proven myself, I figured my self-esteem would rise again. Of course, this wasn't necessarily the case, but subconsciously, this idea somehow ingrained itself in my psyche after sharing my plan with Devon.

There was no competition or concept similar to ours in Jamaica. My research had revealed that water was a natural resource available in abundance in Portland, yet the water wasn't being adequately distributed. I was thrilled to also find out that this particular water source was naturally alkaline, which no other bottled water brand on the market could claim. We decided to capitalize on this fact, which is how we began to market our brand.

When an individual consumes naturally alkaline spring water, it restores the pH balance in the body. In other words, it neutralizes the acidity of the body caused by a bad or subpar diet, stress, and air pollution. All in all, naturally alkaline spring water was what our new company would offer consumers.

A few weeks later, Devon and I were driving to the north coast by ourselves. Our car rides had ended in arguments for months, but this car ride was different. We had something in common that we could discuss with exuberance and excitement – the bottled water project. Along the way, we stopped at a gas station to get some refreshments, including a bottle of water. But the station didn't carry bottled water. I bought a bottle with clear liquid, unsure of what was inside but when I tried a sip, I spat it out immediately. The remnants in my mouth tasted of an overpowering sweetness; the drink was full of sugar, and some more sugar.

Before I threw out the bottle, I noticed the name on the label: "Viva," which translates to "live" in English. Devon noticed the branding on the bottle as well.

I held the bottle in my hand outside the station as I told Devon, "We need a word to summarize what our bottled water product means. Water is such an important part of sustaining life, which we often take for granted. Also, the human body is made up of 70% water (nasa.gov). When we don't drink enough water, it leads to dehydration and a host of other health problems, including fatigue, headaches, dry skin, abdominal cramps, and so much more."

Devon silently nodded away, taking in everything I was saying outside of our parked SUV. Suddenly, he looked at me intently and with the biggest smile I had ever seen on his face, he blurted out, "Lifespan."

I covered my mouth with both hands and jumped up and down, hugging and kissing him.

"You're brilliant!" I shouted. A few patrons glanced our way, looking at us in confusion, but I didn't care. We were a team again. A unit. Two beings molded into one. And we had just come up with our new business name together. In January 2005, Lifespan Company Limited, producer of Lifespan Spring Water – which has a pH level ranging between 7.9-8.4 – was officially established, and we couldn't have been prouder of this achievement.

Chapter 20

The Business Plan

Jamaica is divided into three counties, which are subdivided into fourteen parishes. My family and I resided in the parish of Portland at the time, which was very laid back. We only had basic commercial activities in these small towns; medium-sized businesses existed in the capital along with a small tourism and hospitality industry.

Our first step in making Lifespan come to fruition was to look at the natural resources available and come up with a plan. The rainfall we experienced in the Blue Mountains was quite frequent, and we as a community also had dozens of rivers, streams, and springs. Basically, there was no shortage of water.

There are different types of drinking water. What differentiates water is its origin, its mineral composition and the method of filtration and disinfection utilized to arrive at a finished product which meets the required standards for drinking water.

Lifespan sourced its water from a spring, which overflows from an aquifer deep in the Blue Mountains of Jamaica. On the potential for hydrogen scale, it ranges between 7.9 and 8.4, making

Lifespan naturally alkaline, the purest type of drinking water, and the best for the human body to ingest. I saw the development and distribution of this product as an enhancement of health. I knew that my community would be happier, stronger, and healthier once we could get this bottled water into the hands of consumers on the island. The blood, sweat, and tears we poured into Lifespan over the first several years were a reflection of my own core values and how I wanted to lead the company. I was giddy with excitement and overjoyed at the fact that I had found a way to benefit my own community in my home country.

After coming up with the initial plan, we were introduced to an attorney by a friend of Devon's who drafted the necessary documents so we could officially incorporate the business. I also created a manufacturing processing manual which I presented to a panel at the Ministry of Health. The members sat there silently as I went over the process plan, I had spent months creating. They seemed extraordinarily impressed with the idea of a naturally alkaline bottled spring water, and the process to maneuver natural resources into these water bottles.

While I researched equipment, we needed for the production of bottled water, I asked Devon to find the proper land with the spring water source needed to carry out our plan. We initially anticipated that getting land would be a simple process, but that's not how it worked out. Finding the land was easy but gaining legal access to the land was much more of a challenge. We found a perfect spot right along a stream in Spring Garden where multiple spring water sources flowed and converged into a stream. The land was owned by the government, so we submitted an application to lease or purchase, whichever would be considered. But soon after, several small farmers began applying for the same land. In the meantime, Devon began to clean and farm the land – skills he developed on his own through his own research, trials and error – but we weren't sure this was going to work out. We didn't feel like fighting daily with squatters, and when we asked the government about the other farmers, we weren't given much of a response at all. This led us to believe that we needed to find another land source, just in case our plans for our current one didn't pan out.

While I pursued acquiring the land in Spring Garden, Devon worked on an alternative plan. We found another piece of land close by in Kildare, with a water source which wasn't the same quality as our water source on the Spring Garden land. Since Devon knew the original owners, who resided in Kingston at the time, we went to see them with a proposal to lease this land, which went through.

I grabbed a hold of the lease agreement and smiled fervently. Our business plan was coming to fruition, and our dreams were becoming our reality as a family.

I knew that both water sources needed proper testing to get approval from the Water Resource Authority; we needed a license to abstract water from the spring. It took weeks, as most government agencies do in my experience, yet we still didn't have a plant or equipment. Though Devon and I had worked together on leasing the right equipment, the shipment was delayed several times over. On top of that, the Jamaican tax department needed to be notified that while we had a new business, it wasn't quite operational yet, and so I wrote six monthly letters.

The equipment consisting of a semi-automated rinser, filler, cap tightener, conveyors, coder, tank, pumps, and a water testing kit was purchased from a company in the USA. The owner of the company had sold the business, and the new owner was still trying to sort out the orders the previous owner had left her. It came to the point where I legally threatened her, in writing, that I would report the company to the fair-trading commission; I had already paid for my equipment, and the intended delivery date had passed by a longshot. The woman reacted quickly and positively, apologising profusely and throwing in some additional complimentary items. Prior to that, we applied to the Bureau of Standards and the Ministry of Health for the requisite registrations, and after the equipment arrived and was installed, they were granted.

With the equipment on its way, Devon decided to go by the leased land in Kildare to make the preparations for when the equipment arrived. He constructed a shed to be able to pump water to a tank on a truck, which was then transported to the facility fifteen minutes away in St. Mary.

While he was working on the shed one day, a man came up to him with papers and said, "You've been served," and walked away anonymously. Devon was confused and baffled, as we had no idea what the papers were. He opened the papers to find that the owners of the neighbouring land viewed us as trespassing. He immediately dropped his tools, got in his car, and found the correct leasing documentation. Devon drove to the neighbour's house, finding the front gate unlocked.

"Hello?" He knocked loudly.

A man answered the door grumpily and with a miserable expression on his face.

"Can I help you? Who the hell are you coming here in the middle of the day?"

Devon took a breath and knew this was going to be a tough conversation.

"Sir," Devon stated calmly, "we have a lease agreement. Here's the documentation."

The neighbour snatched the paper's egregiously out of Devon's hands as he fumbled through it, page by page. He suddenly shoved the papers back to Devon with a look of disgust on his face.

"This won't work for us," he said, and slammed the door in front of Devon's face.

A few weeks later, we began the court proceedings, which found that there were, in fact, some geographic changes to how the water flowed through that particular piece of land. A small part of the land we had leased legally belonged to this neighbour, and even though we had no idea at the time, the plan was to erect a pump house on the site of this land. To make matters worse and more confusing, the bank had repossessed the land from the original owners, now former owners, who leased us the land, so the lease wasn't able to be held up in a court of law. Years earlier, the land was actually auctioned off and owned by someone else entirely, who wasn't even at these court proceedings. Luckily, these neighbours took pity upon our situation and agreed to settle with us, leading us back to square one. This time around, we did our due diligence and waited on the government to approve our application before starting construction at the Spring Garden location.

Since we didn't have official possession of the land at Spring Garden yet, we needed to come up with an alternative plan of action. Devon physically constructed a 1200 square foot building to house the plant ten miles away on my father's 42-acre property in St. Mary. Throughout this difficult time, Devon grumbled to me constantly, asserting that, "I didn't know what I was doing" and, "How could I run a business if I couldn't even lease land properly?" I ignored his demeaning comments, which I knew he didn't truly mean, and I persevered. I was driven and determined to make Lifespan work, despite these first few hoops we needed to jump through.

Armed with a Water Abstraction License from the Water Resource Authority, for the first five years, we hired trucks to transport the water daily from Portland to St. Mary. Devon would wake up in the early hours of the morning before daybreak and go to the source to pump the water and transport it to the plant. We started on our experimentation runs and did the necessary water analysis of the product until we were satisfied it was time to start trading.

Branding the bottled water was the next step before we were able to start trading and distributing. I had a few initial ideas for the logo and label, and I inquired about the cost to engage an advertising agency. After making several of these phone calls and receiving no leads, I finally spoke to a director of an advertising company, who asked me what my budget was.

"I don't have a budget," I told him verbatim. "I'm looking to hire a graphic designer to assist me with designing a logo and label for my new bottled water company."

Silence echoed on the other side of the line, only for a moment.

"Listen, let me give you some free advice," the man stated. "If you engage my agency, or any other one, it's going to cost you a pretty penny. We're talking about thousands of dollars. Maybe hundreds of thousands. And you're a start-up, I get that. Let me give you the name of a graphic designer who works for my company. She's a freelancer, and she does this type of work regularly."

I thanked him and immediately called the freelancer, Flavia, who answered right away.

"Flavia? Hi, yes," I started to say. "A director from Chasm gave me your information. Can I give you a concept for what I'm visualizing for my company, and could you come up with some designs for me? How does this work?"

Flavia spoke quickly and quoted me a reasonable price, along with a very reasonable timeframe. The turnaround time was about two weeks, and I paid less than $10,000 for the work. Although the design was not exactly what I wanted, we were nearing the launch date of Lifespan, and so I decided to use the design she produced, with the knowledge that I could do a redesign and fine-tune the brand image later on. Before the launch, I printed labels and purchased bottles, caps, as well as cartons from local suppliers in Kingston, transporting everything back in our pickup truck to the plant.

On June 1, 2006, we loaded our pick-up truck with Lifespan Spring Water and stopped at every single shop we saw. Some of the shop owners purchased the water to sell, and some didn't. But we kept going, no matter their initial response. We talked with managers at local supermarkets, who informed us that they would never sell our product because "consumers don't know about it, so they won't buy it." Some were kinder than others and told us to try again another time. That first day, we sold about ten cases of our brand-new product. Devon's mother was the very first person who purchased a case of water, and my sister was the second. We loved counting on our family to support our vision, dreams, and goals as a unit. Again, my drive came into play, and I didn't care what other people said about my new product. I only concentrated on the people who said "yes" to us, not the ones who said "no" in disbelief. I knew this would be a popular product and in high demand sooner rather than later, and that I would be proven right.

Chapter 21

The Constraints

Besides the fact that I wanted to create a career for myself, I also wanted to empower my community. My personal goal was to produce a healthy product and distribute it to as many individuals as possible. I knew that I could help others, and myself, in the community by making available to consumers our naturally alkaline spring water. While a part of me missed seeing Milan and Elizabeth as often as I used to, I knew they were being taken care of by Dorrette. My office was at home, so during the days I had office work I could still see my children and check on them. Despite all of the other issues we had – the equipment, the neighbour taking us to court, and more – our biggest constraint was finding capital for the company. In Jamaica, lending money was completely different than in the USA. Years ago, Jamaican banks preferred to lend you money for a new car; they weren't so inclined to lend money for start-ups and it still remains the same. At the time, there weren't any venture capitalists, and so our only option was to borrow money from relatives and friends to raise capital. My sister helped us immensely, allowing us to use her property title to secure a business loan, which we paid back in over a year and returned the title to her. We did this due to our own housing situation, which was complicated at the time. Although we owned our house, we didn't have the title. The house was built on land owned by Devon's uncle, but before the title transfer was set in motion, his uncle passed away. I retained a lawyer to settle the matter, but it took many years before we received the proper title documentation.

The second biggest constraint was the human capital available. The talent pool consisted of young people who were both inexperienced and underqualified, and we had a very difficult time training and hiring the right people for positions, which is why Devon, and I took on so many responsibilities, too. Although I took the lead on decision-making in most areas of Lifespan, I didn't give myself a title at the time. When I introduced myself to a new supplier, for instance, I gave them my name and Lifespan's name, but no other title. I suppose I wasn't sure what to call myself at the time, other than a director. I hadn't known any other female CEOs growing up in Jamaica, and so the thought of calling myself the Chief Executive Officer didn't cross my mind.

Our family lives were also very much intertwined with Lifespan. My relationship with Devon blossomed, and we had never been stronger as a couple. We spent more time together in these early years than we had at any other time throughout our relationship. Devon was my biggest supporter, and I was his as well. We encouraged each other to ask for help. We made sure that both of us felt happy with the business decisions we were making, and we never went anywhere without each other. While Devon drove, I made the necessary calls each and every day. Devon and I were at every single meeting together, whether we met with our suppliers, accountants, the bank, or anyone else. If I were dealing with accounting, Devon would oversee the loading of materials. If we were doing route sales, I would engage the customer and, when the order was confirmed, Devon would take the goods to the customer. We weren't able to hire additional employees at the time due to cash constraints, so both of us wore many hats in those early years. Due to my prior experiences, I was in charge of operations, sales, and administration, while Devon was responsible for maintenance, logistics, and engineering projects.

We would go over the next day's plans late in the evening to ensure all responsibilities were met. There are no cut-off hours when you own your own business. We worked late into the night almost daily, yet we tried to mix in some fun as well. When time permitted, we'd have a sit-down lunch together and promised one another we wouldn't answer our phones for twenty minutes, just to be in each other's company. Occasionally, and only if we had completed our tasks for the day in Kingston, we would catch a movie before returning to Portland.

For the first time in a long time, I was able to see us as a team again. A unit. Together, we were ridiculed constantly and were both forced to rise up, counting on our self-esteem to take us higher and higher. Relatives and acquaintances would remark, "Why the hell are you going into the bottled water business?! The market is saturated!"

When I was visiting my mother-in-law one day, I bumped into Devon's brother Maur who was sitting on the steps of the balcony. Without any prompting, he said to me, "Listen, Sandy, I'm very familiar with the bottled water business… I have some friends who own one of these businesses and let me tell you this; this bottle water business won't go anywhere."

Then he added viciously, "You are wasting your time… there's no way your business will be a success."

I smiled at him and walked away.

Kill them with kindness, I thought to myself.

Other relatives decided to remark on my parenting and my choices to have someone else help raise my babies.

"Shouldn't you be at home with your babies? What the hell are you doing working while your children are so young?" they'd say with concern in their voices.

I did feel mum-guilt at times, but I also knew that by starting this company, I would be more fulfilled than I ever had been staying at home with my babies. I no longer needed to solve math equations in the middle of the day to challenge myself. Adult conversations were more prominent in my life than they had been since before Beth was born. Devon and I were one again, holding hands on a mission to better the community by distributing the healthiest bottled water Jamaica had ever seen.

*

In 2006, bottled water sales grew every week by significant percentages. We knew we needed more financial capital as well as human capital. Devon borrowed funds from his brother David, who, at the time, still lived in the US. He sent us a golden ticket – a credit card convenience check for $10,000 USD; at the time, the exchange rate with Jamaican currency was just over $60. After Devon exchanged the check, he gave me a portion which was a grand total of $300,000 JMD, which was used to purchase more bottles immediately.

David soon returned to Jamaica, and Devon sat me down to ask me a serious question.

"Sandy," he said. "Listen, I really think David could be an asset to Lifespan. What'd you say we give him a try? We've been working together, and we're family. It's been so difficult to find good people to hire, and we know David will do a good job. I know we have Warren to assist, but David has management experience. We'll give him tasks and responsibilities, and he'll fulfill them."

I was weary at the mere thought of working with David. Though we didn't necessarily have a bad relationship, I had never worked with him on anything before. I had reservations, mostly because in the past he seemed dissatisfied upon seeing me at the guesthouse whenever I visited Devon; it made me feel uncomfortable, like I was not welcomed there. Hesitation overtook me, and I stood there in stone-cold silence.

"Please, Sandy, I really think this is a good idea."

Devon was pleading with me now. Perhaps I was silent for longer than I had initially thought. I took a deep breath and finally spoke.

"Okay, fine, Devon, you win this one," I told him. Looking back now, I know I only agreed to this premonition because I so badly wanted to please Devon. Though we worked side-by-side together, there was this longing for him to be happy. I desired happiness myself, yet I also desperately wanted Devon to know that I was his rock and his ultimate support as well.

And so, David became the Production Manager of Lifespan, which paid him $15,000 JMD per week. Devon and I ensured we paid both him and Warren, but because our cash flow was subpar, we weren't able to pay ourselves a salary still.

After several months, David purchased a pick-up truck of his own and began to assist with sales and delivery on the Port Antonio route on Wednesdays. By this time, Lifespan had three routes on a weekly basis: Port Antonio, Kingston, and the Northcoast. Soon enough, it was apparent that the pick-up trucks weren't sufficient to support the load we needed to distribute, since our orders were dramatically increasing. We sometimes had to drive both pick-up trucks simultaneously and make multiple trips to fulfill orders. Rain was our worst-case scenario, since the boxes would get wet in the back of the pick-up trucks, despite our many attempts to cover them with a tarp.

I walked into our bank the following morning in Kingston and asked if we could have a business loan to purchase a box body truck. The man looked at me with a confused expression.

"You drive a truck?" he asked incredulously. I wondered how often he asked this question to my male counterparts.

"I will get a license and learn, but that's not what I'm asking today," I responded in kind.

"What do you need it for?"

The banker played with a small ball in his hands, rolling it back and forth on his desk, barely making eye contact with me.

"We can finance 60% of commercial loans," he said bluntly and without any remorse. "That's all."

Would he have been more likely to finance the truck more if Devon had asked?

I walked out of there, while thoughts swarmed my mind. I already knew this wouldn't work because we couldn't finance the other 40%.

I walked into the second bank we banked with the next day in St. Ann, and the manager there treated me more like a businesswoman. He offered us 75%, which was significantly better than the first offer, yet we didn't know where we could get the other 25% from.

After leaving that office, the following day I drove back to the first bank which was located in New Kingston to see the loan officer again.

"You're back," he said casually, and unsurprisingly. "Change your mind?"

I told him about the other bank's offer. He sat up straight in his chair and cleared his throat.

"Well, I suppose we could give you 90%, but that's my highest offer," he stated.

I shook his hand enthusiastically.

"It's a deal."

We purchased our first truck, a Chinese-made Foton Forland 3 Ton Box Body Truck. When it arrived at the plant, all four of us were giddy with excitement. This was a huge step in expanding the Lifespan brand. Devon drove the truck for the first few weeks until we hired a driver – this gave us so much more flexibility and bandwidth to expand our distribution network, as demand grew and grew.

Devon and David did most of their work at the factory to ensure production was running smoothly, but on Wednesdays, we ran the Port Antonio route together. These adventures allowed us to bond further in our common cause – we wanted more and more individuals to drink healthier water. I continued to keep myself busy with work. Distractions were the best way for me to continue to cope with Devon's previous betrayal. While Devon and I were back on good terms still, the thought of him being with someone else would creep into my psyche late at night. When this happened, I shook off those negative thoughts and found something to do for Lifespan. I didn't allow myself time to reflect on these feelings, because I couldn't bear the pain that had tried to resurface. Work allowed me to focus on my drive and my passion to help others, and I relished this opportunity.

*

After purchasing the Foton Forland Truck, our bottled water sales skyrocketed in Portland and St. Mary. We slowly began to venture into other areas as well, including Ocho Rios, St. Ann. One day, a retailer called me and ordered 150 cases. I jumped up out of my chair and shouted at Devon and David immediately after hanging up the phone. We were grinning ear to ear, as this was the largest order we had to date.

The following morning, Devon drove the cases to Ocho Rios, and I sat next to him in the middle. I spoke with the retailer, who didn't seem disingenuous at the time, and unloaded all 150 cases. Instead of paying us that day, she wanted us to come back the following day with another 150 cases. We obliged willingly, believing that she would, in fact, pay for both orders the next day. The same routine occurred, though, and she asked for another 150 cases, making her total 450 cases. I was hesitant but wanted to believe her. I've always believed in the goodness of others and couldn't fathom why someone would try to steal a new product on the market, especially bottled water. Devon was getting extremely suspicious at this point, too. On the third day in a row, we went to this retailer, but we didn't unload these cases this last time.

I approached the retailer for payment instead.

"Ms. Moses, how are you today?" I said kindly, not wanting to sound suspicious. "We have brought you another 150 cases of bottled water as ordered, and we delivered 300 cases previously, but I see you have none in stock in your storeroom… we're not able to unload this batch until our payment is received. Is the check ready?"

She stood unwavering, then said, "Let me get the payment for you, I'll be back in a bit."

But she never came back.

I found another worker, who had told me she "had left the facility and wouldn't be back for a while," which was extraordinarily suspicious. When I asked about payment, I was told to direct all payment questions to Ms. Moses, who had since left.

Devon and I left the retailer in silence with our 150 cases of product. But we had already lost 300 cases. We also realized that if Ms. Moses had initially asked us for the amount she actually wanted, we could have made less trips, as the truck could fit 350-400 cases at a time. We would also be out 450 cases instead.

I learned a great deal about business that day. For some more experienced business women and men, they already know to ask for at least a partial payment up front before distributing a product or service. But Devon and I didn't know about this methodology at the time. From then on, I was not afraid to ask about the method of payment and how the payment would be transferred. Never leave anything hanging in the balance, especially when it comes to money and finances, and always try to upsell from the beginning when the opportunity presents itself. Have clear boundaries from the start of a working relationship, and these boundaries should never be crossed.

The good that came from this experience was the benefit of the brand becoming known in the area as a result of Ms. Moses distributing it to her customers. Shortly after, the retailers and wholesalers in that area started ordering the product on a weekly basis.

Chapter 22

Spring Garden

Our factory in Spring Garden was nearing completion in 2011. After being on the road for an entire day visiting customers and taking orders, I recall seeing a truck that we owned parked in its usual spot. At this time, we had two trucks to carry out logistics, as our distribution and demand had increased in the past few years.

As I was driving past the entrance of the road to our old factory, which was still operational but closed for the day, I saw a truck leaving the property that mirrored the one I had just seen at the new factory. I did a double take. Tiredness crept up into my eyelids, and I was completely puzzled by this scenario. I questioned what I had seen at our new factory, and so I called Devon.

"Are you nuts, Sandy? Of course you're not seeing things straight," he said to me. "Didn't you just leave the truck at the new factory?"

"Yeah, I know I did. I know for a fact that I saw it there, parked," I told him. "Anyways, I'm sure it's fine, maybe I'm just seeing things."

"Yeah probably."

He hung up, and I felt worse than I did before I talked with him. I didn't have a chance to think much about this, though, because I had to rush to another customer to collect our payment before they closed for the day.

Later on, I found out that one of our employees – the brother of Devon's best friend – teamed up with our haulage contractor, took a load of products to a customer and sold them at a 50% discount; they pocketed the money for themselves and never told a soul at Lifespan. Devon and I learned that these two men were corroborating for months, and our booking records were inaccurate, as well. When the customer who purchased this load migrated to a different country, he called me and confessed this story to me. He said he wanted to clear his conscience, and I forgave him, accepting his apology. I have always been cognizant of human imperfections when it comes to indiscipline and greed. Though I find these actions and behaviors intolerant, I find that it is imperative in life to reach a place of solace and forgiveness rather than bitterness. Yet there were more lessons I needed to learn about people, trust, and respect.

The same haulage contractor who stole from us was also the contractor, at the time, who hauled our bottles from our bottle supplier. Back then, we supplied our labels to be applied to the bottles before they went out for distribution, and we maintained a respectful working relationship with the staff of our bottle and cap supplier. One time, we even supplied one of the staff who owned a small shop with five-gallon bottled water at a 50% discount, just because we had the ability to do so, and we wanted to help another small business.

But that staff member wasn't so kind, in the end. He refilled up to twenty-two bottles per week, and that number dramatically increased as the weeks turned into months. He claimed the bottles were for his shop, which he owned outside of his job at this factory. I discovered, much later, that this employee teamed up with the haulage contractor to steal our bottles and caps. They would fill our bottles with the five-gallon bottles of water and would sell a case in downtown Kingston at half price. It was a similar scheme that the haulage contractor tried to pull off with Devon's brother's best friend. We finally understood why we had an excessive amount of money that we owed to our bottle suppliers, which strained our relationship.

These situations that the haulage contractor decidedly put us in created extreme risk and extraordinary losses for Lifespan, though I learned important and valuable lessons from them. I was forced to make decisions that would propel Lifespan further on the path to success, meaning we would have a positive profit margin, and Devon and I would both earn a salary, which took seven years. We took a small salary on paper before this seventh year but did not actually see a penny until our seventh year in business and the amount was still less than everyone else employed by the company. The clothes I wore were mostly from before I came back to Jamaica, except for the branded shirts I wore when representing the company in public. I did laundry several times a week, simply because I didn't have enough clothing to make it through seven days. I put every penny I earned back into the company. Clothing, jewelry, going out to eat, or any other activity that didn't have to do with Lifespan was no longer important to me at all. I chuckle now as I think about this, considering I was once a fashion model, obsessed with clothes. I had mastered the idea of living frugally and sacrificing my own well-being and personal routines became habitual. I needed to ensure that all our company bills were paid on time; this was significantly more important to me than the latest design.

*

I started approaching different distributors to carry our brand, as we did not have the capital nor the infrastructure in place to cover the entire island. We went with a few smaller ones at first, and as we grew, we signed with major distributors to dispense our locally sourced water products.

While Lifespan progressed through the years, there were times where I began to get uncomfortable with our major distributor. I felt they were inconsistent with how they were operating. Though there was a set monthly target, they were performing inconsistently; often below our targets, and our weekly sales audits across the trades revealed that merchandising and sales follow up were poor. However, their explanation was that it had to do with the customer ordering pattern and a decline in consumer spending. Yet our survey indicated that while the inflation rate would rise and fall, no matter where the market hit, the consumer demand for bottled water continued to rise. Having the necessary distribution is a critical part of a bottled water company; if the distributor's performance was below expectations, this would automatically have a negative impact on the business. Years later, during the 2020 worldwide pandemic, I recognized there were even more constraints on operating companies, and so we all had to navigate this new norm together.

We still retained our own territory, and by 2014, we began exporting to other countries, including the UK, Cayman, Antigua, Bermuda, and the British Virgin Islands. Lifespan became my daily obsession. I lived and breathed Lifespan. I felt fortunate to have this opportunity to continue building the Lifespan brand. When I initially came up with the idea of Lifespan, I didn't know how complex it would be to receive loans for different aspects of the business.

Due to government regulations and bureaucratic novices, it took us five years to acquire the land at Spring Garden. The letters and calls I had sent pestering the National Land Agency actually worked. The employees all knew me by my first name. The agency eventually approved my application in 2010 which gave us the green light to build the new plant by the source.

Simultaneously, another company contracted Lifespan to co-pack another bottled water brand for them. They had to pay us a large sum of money at the time the agreement was signed, which happened to be on September 1, my birthday. Weeks prior to this contract popping up, we received a loan from the Jamaica Business

Development Corporation (JBDC). We now had enough funds to build our plant on forty acres of land with seven springs at our disposal, yet we only needed to abstract water from one spring at a fraction of its flow rate. The JBDC loan combined with proceeds from the co-packing deal only allowed us to construct the warehouse, though. There was a cap on the JBDC loan, since it was designed to fulfill the capital needs of a very small business, which wasn't my overall vision for Lifespan. We still needed additional funds to upgrade our electricity supply, upgrade equipment to increase production capacity, as well as working capital to purchase more packaging materials. Our next step was to use our property title to collateralize a loan with the bank to expand the business.

*

I was doing my usual visits with all my suppliers once a week, paying for packaging materials and placing new orders. These payments were generally substantial, amounting to hundreds of thousands of dollars monthly. Our bottle supplier at the time would constantly ask us to double up our purchase order, and they'd hold the bottles until we needed them. We began this practice, which lasted for several years. Yet more often than not, this particular bottle supplier would call me and tell me I only had twenty-four hours to collect this extra shipment due to space constraints. I'd constantly feel rushed to collect the shipment, and, of course, I felt I needed to do this myself. I didn't care to train anyone to take over this task at the time, and so this ate a half-day of my time at least every time the supplier called to notify me. Occasionally, the supplier would send over the bottles with a trucker we were familiar with, which I thought was a kind gesture.

One day in January 2013, I received a curious letter from an attorney on behalf of our bottle supplier, indicating that we should wind up our company and pay them. I immediately called the managing director, asking what this letter was about, assuming it must be some sort of mistake in their billing department as the past week I had paid them a substantial amount.

"It's no mistake, Nayana, I assure you," he told me coldly. This was a shock, as I had considered him a friend and trusted person in my business negotiations. "Our board of directors is putting pressure on us," he continued, "it's now completely out of our hands."

"But we're paying customers—"

He hung up on me without another word and didn't let me finish. I held the phone in my hand as confusion spread across my face. I knew I needed to solve yet another problem with Lifespan, and I also knew that getting the legal team involved would cost thousands of dollars on the company's behalf.

After looking through some more documentation, I realized that the bottle supplier had acquired the land next door to us. The company was trying to force us into a position to dispose of Lifespan by putting us in a position of not being able to pay them within their required timeframe. They wanted to build a bottling facility and have access to Lifespan's spring. I wouldn't let that happen.

I kindly asked via email – indicating a proper paper trail, of course – to send an overall account statement. They obliged willingly, which I took as a good sign. On the statements, I noticed that the supplier would apply Lifespan's current payments to the newer invoices and left older invoices unpaid, even though Lifespan's records showed that the old invoices had already been taken care of. On top of this, I discovered that some of the invoices they stated on the document weren't even in our own billing system at Lifespan. I looked through our supply from the previous week and noticed that the number of supplies delivered was less than what was accounted for on the invoice.

We did take legal action against them after they sued Lifespan for a breach of contract. In our suit, we stated that the supplier deliberately and intentionally forced us to take bottles from them, under the pretense that their warehouse was full, with the sole intent to drive up our account balance. They knew that we would not be able to pay them within the usual thirty-day timeframe outlined in the terms of our contract. At the time, we had a verbal agreement in which they allowed us extra time to pay, given the fact that the quantities of bottles they had were higher than the amount we initially ordered each week. I was grateful for this type of leverage, and we had gladly accepted, yet I was unaware of the ulterior motives behind their generosity at the time.

After years of being entangled in this lawsuit, both sides agreed to have the court appoint an auditor. We had already called witnesses, former employees, contractors, and more, but it was never-ending and extraordinarily exhausting. Before the case went to trial, we agreed to pay the difference of what was owed to them, whether we received the bottles or not. The court asked us to propose a set monthly amount until the total bill was paid off, which took years. We dropped our suit as well, and I celebrated, knowing that this legal battle was behind Lifespan. Again, I felt I was being tested in order to prove not only how strong I was, and what I was capable of handling, but also how I was able to forgive others.

Despite the lawsuit entanglement, the same bottle supplier still proceeded to build a factory neighbouring our own, and they launched an inferior brand of bottled water. Through advertisements, they claimed to have a similar product to Lifespan due to its geographic location. However, our source of water and their source couldn't have been more different; the way in which the water was extracted, along with its mineral composition, were opposing one another. Whilst our water source originated directly from a spring flowing from the Blue Mountains, their source came from a well which they dug all the way to sea level before they could access water. That is why it was important for them to try and get our spring. Still, I let this slide because I knew Lifespan would continue to see success. If someone else wanted to start a bottled water company, so let them, I decided. Let them see the work, the tireless hours, and the effort that goes into creating a powerful, sustainable, and healthy brand of bottled water. I no longer see other bottled water companies as competition; instead, I praise them for wanting to commit to the health and richness of our world by helping thousands of people have access to clean drinking water. I already knew that Lifespan stood apart and consumers who tried our product would eventually tell the difference for themselves, as not all waters are created equal.

We were also faced with fierce competition from the goliaths in the business world. A very large corporation in Jamaica acquired a majority stake in our main competitor, and they also launched a bargain brand. The first thing they did was negotiate with the largest wholesale club in Jamaica to have the Lifespan brand removed from its shelf. Consumer choice, need, feedback, or business returns was not a consideration. This company sadly claimed that their bottled water had the same pH balance as Lifespan's, which was false advertising. They targeted the Lifespan brand and tried their best to relegate us into a failed position.

When we discovered what this company was doing, I gathered my quintessential team members to strategize. We discussed how we could remain relevant and visible in the eyes of our valued consumers, which was no easy task. Misinformation became rampant in the bottled water world, and the lack of government policy allowed for continuous misrepresentation on labels. Instead of stooping down to this company's level, we decided to thrive with authenticity, and our consumers loved it. As a result, Lifespan stood apart from the competition as the only naturally alkaline spring water of its kind on the market. We maintained the brand's quality while achieving the highest international quality award multiple times, putting Jamaica on the world stage in the bottled water business.

Throughout the years, Lifespan continues to set a trend for other businesses. I am constantly encouraged to raise our bar even higher in terms of where we buy our supplies, our training manuals, our internal systems, our employees, and more. As of the writing of this book, Lifespan is the only brand and facility in the local bottled water industry to be certified by the National Sanitation Foundation (NSF) and to be a member of the International Bottled Water Association (IBWA). We have also won the grand gold quality award from the internationally acclaimed Monde Selection multiple years in a row, which speaks to the quality and premium status of our brand.

Chapter 23

Female Marginalization

When I started the business, there were so many moments when I felt like giving up but still, I persisted. At times, I became so exhausted with all that was coming at me but giving up was never an option. Besides my family, many people depended on me, including hundreds of employees, and I had to inspire them to be strong in the face of adversity.

Whenever I experienced a setback, I took a minute or two to wince at what had occurred, then immediately proceeded to dust myself off. I had a vision for what the Lifespan brand could become, and I followed it to a tee. There were many times where I thought of giving up, I will admit. My inner critic would come alive in those moments, taunting me, and explaining why I wasn't good enough, or why I should quit. Those moments took me down a dark path, yet I was able to pull myself out and see positivity and light once again.

In 2012, we held a launch for Lifespan at the Spanish Court Hotel in Kingston. I was elated that we had signed two Olympians as our brand ambassadors, and my team had worked hard to make this dream become a reality. A few of our suppliers came, as well as the press, the athletes, distribution representatives, and the Sports Minister. The crowd was networking, with small groups gathered in conversation, and I walked through stopping to welcome and chit chat along the way. I came upon a group and there was this particular man who proceeded to blurt out in front of those gathered in the group: "Why the hell are you here, Nayana Williams?" His remark was cynical, letting me know what little respect he had for me. "Where the hell is your husband?" he added. "Shouldn't he be present at his own business launch? What do you have to do with Lifespan anyways?"

The group grew silent as this man's voice overpowered others in the audience. There were only about five people present in total, however the crowd outside this group was large enough to drown out his remarks. To this man, being a woman did not qualify me to represent my own company, something that would continue to be prominent as the Lifespan brand grew larger and larger.

I ignored his demeaning comments, along with the presence of others in the crowd, and I moved on with a smile on my face. It was true that Devon didn't attend – he trusted me to run the business and wasn't particularly fond of going to media-sponsored events. I felt my inner critic asking questions when the man spoke, but again, I brushed off his words and continued to pursue my own belief in what I was creating for my community, and for the world.

My focus, attitude, fearlessness, and faith in what I was doing is what carried me through these doubts. I knew I had to be smarter and work harder to continue to build my dream business, especially because I'm a woman, and there weren't many female CEOs in Jamaica. While I only cared about someone's character and intelligence, others cared a lot more about what that person looked like, and what gender they were. Being a female in the business world didn't phase me. Even though I was the one mainly managing the company, from the beginning I wanted Devon to be the CEO, because males were more readily accepted in our society in leadership roles, but he eventually declined. Therefore, I was left with the reins, so I took charge of the responsibility head on, and I grew the business. I wanted to be an example for not only my team, but also for my young, bright female employees who one day could rise up and become CEOs themselves. In the world of entrepreneurship, there are always obstacles. The tricky part is to find a way to get through each obstacle and remain standing tall on your two feet; be strong, let the world know that you're still here, and your business will still thrive.

I was met with trepidation as a woman for many years, despite my title as CEO. One time, Devon and I were meeting with the managing director and others of a company that supplied Lifespan with some of our packaging materials. Out of seven people sitting around a large, white table by Gloria's seafood restaurant in Port Royal, I was the only woman. This company really wanted to form an alliance with Lifespan to create another brand for the export market. Their oral presentation was impressive, outlining how the parent company would be structured and how share ownership would be divided. They mentioned four parts with Devon Williams of Lifespan owning a portion, not "Devon and Nayana Williams." My name was never mentioned at any time. It was like I was an invisible anchor in the water, floating underneath the surface.

They decided to include me only when outlining my own responsibilities, where they were telling me what I needed to do and what information I needed to provide to them. They treated me as Devon's administrative assistant instead of the CEO of Lifespan, which bothered me greatly. I felt my cheeks get hot, yet I kept a smile on my face. I knew that if I talked back, I would just be demeaning my character. So, I sat there silently, listening intently, and allowed them to make whatever plans they wanted. Devon noticed my name wasn't associated with the title of CEO either by giving me a glance and pinching my thigh, something we started doing in meetings when Lifespan first started. At the end of the meeting, a sheet of paper was thrown across the table towards me, while another sheet was gently placed and maneuvered in front of Devon. Even the men's body language helped me realize that they would never see me as one of them, only because of my gender. I smiled and told them I would think about this decision, leaving the piece of paper blank, and walked away. Devon got up and escorted me to our SUV, and when the company followed up with us, Devon gently told them we had decided to move in a different direction. It was partially a business decision, and partially a personal decision – they blatantly disregarded a female business leader. Through years of trial and error, a great lesson I learned was that business decisions and personal decisions were often intertwined.

Sticking up for myself as a woman wasn't always easy, yet in order to make Lifespan grow, I knew I needed to grow as an individual and as a leader, paving the way for other future female innovators. For many years, constant demeaning comments were made towards me, even by relatives and immediate family members. I would hear comments, such as, "You have no idea what you are doing" or "You cannot manage this business? We need someone more qualified to handle this business and I should be getting more money, but instead you are paying more people to do what you should be doing. All you do is sit in your air-conditioned office doing what? Or go to meetings with all those men." Women in my life were even more direct, telling me that I should "go back to being with the kids" and that I "had absolutely no place in a man's world" meaning I should not have been running Lifespan.

My capabilities as a woman caused some people to compare me to that of a man, though I did not look or behave in a masculine way. I had to be very strict with managing the company's resources and as a result I would hear time and time again, "You are like a man, controlling like a commander. You want everything for yourself… you are greedy." Yet these same people were reaping attractive rewards from the success of Lifespan under my leadership; they failed to acknowledge this and instead made false assumptions about me, misjudged me and criticized me to my face, as well as to others.

I often felt like I had no support and felt backed up against a wall at times. I did not hold their remarks against them, but it hurt, nonetheless. I realized it was their lack of knowledge and wisdom which prevented them from understanding the different roles and responsibilities in the business. There was nothing I could do about their perceptions or beliefs, as I had no control over their thoughts or actions. Sadly, neither did they see it necessary to try to gain the appropriate knowledge to make more accurate judgements of me. There was also the small-mindedness which got in the way. I only had control over my own thoughts and actions. Trying to clarify their perception would have been futile, as often times people become believers of their own theories without the evidence to back it up. It's like saying we can get ten additional customers in a certain location, but the unknown fact is that there are only five existing prospects at that particular location.

The fact is that my leadership style was more democratic. Though I took the lead when I had to, it was not out of the need to control but more so because most times I was caught in a situation where others around me were indecisive when critical decisions needed to be made. This is what led me to becoming the high-level CEO of Lifespan and not just the founder with a vision.

From the initial stages of the business, I was in charge of financing and banking activities. Upon joining a bank when we started Lifespan, I recognized an employee, named Althea, who would eventually become our business banker. She was a former childhood friend however, we had a falling out in our early twenties. I found out she was pursuing my sister's boyfriend at the time while posing as a friend to her, which didn't sit well with me. After a bad argument, I slowly parted ways with her, as I didn't want to expend energy on someone who thought their immoral actions were absolutely fine.

We didn't really have a choice when she was assigned to our company at the bank. When she saw me, she did a double take and immediately squirmed in her chair. In her dark blue pantsuit, she pretended to flip through some paperwork instead of making eye contact with me.

"I'm busy right now, please come another time," she noted without remorse and without a proper greeting. Later that day, she proceeded to call Devon with a question about Lifespan. No matter how many times Devon directed Althea to me, she continued to call Devon with any new information or questions. This occurred over a period of months, and both Devon and I became sick of the practice. Althea was unable to separate her personal life from her professional life. At first, I thought she was acting this way just because Devon was seen as the primary signatory on our account due to his gender, but I soon realized it was a combination between him being a male as well as Althea's personal grudge against me.

Before I withdrew Lifespan from this particular bank, I requested an informational meeting with the manager, who happened to be a woman.

"I want to let you know why I've decided to withdraw my organization's funds from this bank," I told the woman, who was called Nordia. "Althea was a former childhood friend of mine, and

I'm not sure why she is holding a grudge against me from twenty years ago, but she is."

Nordia looked shocked and a bit confused. She proceeded to listen intently as I outlined more of my experience and the lack of support I was receiving. When I finished my side of the story, Nordia told me that she was married, too, and her husband would pick her up on the weekends.

"We're faced with more hoops to jump through just because of the mere fact that we are women," she stated, and sighed in agreement. "I understand what you're facing, I really do. I'm aware that some of the bankers prefer to speak with male counterparts, even my female employees. It's something I'm trying to change, but it's going to take more time."

She looked directly at me.

"I'm so sorry this happened to you," Nordia said, and it was genuine. "Please reconsider taking your business elsewhere. I will handle your account personally going forward, and Althea won't be in the picture."

I took a moment to take in what she was saying.

Could I trust her?

I decided to try one more time, and I kept Lifespan's funds in that bank. My trust in others would be broken many times over throughout the years, yet Nordia, luckily, hasn't fallen into that category. For a few years after that conversation, Nordia was my reliable, trustworthy banker, and when she was leaving, she introduced me to the incoming bank manager who I also developed a great relationship with.

I continued to manage various aspects of the business, and I learned how to compartmentalize the different roles I had to play in my life, whether they were business-related or personal. The difficulty was not accomplishing all my tasks; it was figuring out how to best use my time and energy on each separate task, so nothing was lost in the mix. Again, I asked myself what my true values were and how I could utilize my values while being disciplined about my work. I attribute my positive growth to my strong value system and my ability to maintain an incredibly powerful work ethic. Rather than a jumble of handwritten notes on post-it notes, I became extraordinarily organized and planned my weeks and months accordingly. I used a notebook and calendar to document everything and referred to it as religiously as the Bible, noting deadlines, payments due, and even personal matters involving my children. I constantly reflected on my own values as a leader and knew that my employees needed to have, or strive to have, the same values as I did. We continued to invest in systems as gaps arose in hiring, training, and managing team members. I also learned a great deal about boundaries during this time period. Reflecting back now, I am stronger than I ever thought I could be, putting boundaries on my time and energy, and possessing the tenacity to ensure the high quality of the Lifespan brand.

While I'm proud of my own achievements within the company, I cannot take all the credit. Devon played a critical role in building the business, and my brother-in-law David was vital to the operation and maintenance of the factory operations, as well as ensuring the product was of the highest quality. While we had disagreements along the way, the three of us wore as many hats as we could muster in order to make Lifespan the brand what it is today. Devon and I had our date nights, but more often than not, dates were few and far between, and they were spontaneous in nature.

Along with Devon and David, I was lucky enough to encounter fantastic employees along the way – some for a season, and some for many years. All of them contributed their intelligence and more dimensions to the company, and I'm forever grateful to them. On the other hand, some employees were not great fits, and their employment threatened to dissolve my entire value system, as well as my confidence that I previously had in myself and in systems that were already in place.

Whilst I am naturally humble about my doings as a business leader and innovator, it was misinterpreted constantly as weakness or stupidity. To this day, I still have relatives wondering why a different person isn't in charge, despite my many successes and achievements. They felt that as a leader I should be more autocratic as that is what being a leader meant to them. I've since realized, though, that I only have control over my own actions. We can't control how others perceive us in leadership roles, and we can't please everyone in our lives. The people who didn't believe in me, and continue to not believe in me, are no longer of my concern. Their mindsets don't match mine; in fact, I've found that their own limiting beliefs directly mirror the words they've spoken to me. I don't hold this notion against them; instead, I move forward, surrounding myself with loving, kind people who do believe in me and are passionate about the Lifespan brand. No stumbling blocks can phase me any longer, though there would be more to come in the journey of Lifespan.

Chapter 24

Empathy for Employees

While David, Devon and I were on good terms the majority of the time, we were still family running a business together, and we didn't always agree on everything. Being a woman, and being myself in general, I interacted with employees, customers, and consumers much differently than Devon and David did. Acknowledging people's personality traits and basic human rights has always been imperative to me; I am known for giving employees multiple opportunities and chances to do things the correct way. I truly believe that all people are inherently good, and I like to believe in justice and fairness for everyone. I often said to myself, "If someone makes a mistake, try to work with them. Help them to be better at what they want to accomplish in their life." But if someone commits a wrongdoing, and there is adequate evidence to substantiate this, then they would have to suffer the consequences, like the haulage contractor. I believe that making assumptions about people and their motives can get you in trouble. Being judgmental can make matters worse, especially within a professional setting.

In the early days of Lifespan, I recognized that I gave too many chances to individuals due to my empathetic nature. For instance, I should not have gone to Ms. Moses three separate times. I should have gone once, and I should have attempted to get paid before distributing that first order of 150 cases. But "should have's" and "could have's" are things of the past, not the present, nor the future.

My "giving chances" mentality came to an abrupt halt when Lifespan could no longer afford my empathetic attitude. I was forced to reach a balance within myself and how I viewed my leadership role at Lifespan. I slowly learned that the majority of our employees lacked the discipline and principles required to carry out their responsibilities, which made me sad. I thought they had potential, but I could no longer worry about training them or pleasing them. Instead, my primary focus needed to be on the business itself, not necessarily on how to help each and every individual working within it. Laziness often became a huge part of their headspace, and more often than not, the first set of "qualified" employees we had at Lifespan wanted to be paid without putting in the work or any effort at all.

Money was a difficult yet necessary topic of discussion with employees. I had several employees who berated me about a senior staff member. They became disgruntled and complained that the senior employee was making a large purchase for the company that wasn't necessary, and the money spent on that should have gone to their own salaries instead. I found it impossibly taxing to deal with employees who had this mindset. Instead of asking how they could help grow the company so we could reach more revenue goals and increase the bottom line so everyone could realize a bonus at the end of the year, they suffered from small-mindedness – they could only see what was right in front of them. They focused on what they did not have versus what they already had – a well-paying job at a new, flourishing company.

Throughout the first fourteen years of the business, the level of talent available was extraordinarily poor. Though hundreds of people were hired and trained, I still felt the need to micromanage their daily responsibilities and tasks. When Lifespan began to grow more and more, I learned that hiring the right people to take over tasks would be extremely important. It felt cumbersome being the CEO and still having to tell employees what to do and how to do it. I found myself having to still make sales calls, follow up on sales orders, order supplies, write checks, personally deliver samples to external labs for testing and set up for promotional events. I was filling in as a promoter at times, doing collections, checking off, taking orders, and interviewing production workers; I had to source equipment parts, request quotations, conduct customer follow ups, troubleshoot production issues and respond to customer complaints, all while still analyzing the company's performance against the budget, and updating the company's strategic plan, as well as all the other many responsibilities I had as the CEO.

We were constantly restructuring the organization, taking away crucial responsibilities from some and handing them over to others who I thought would be more capable of handling a dense workload. The plant employed hundreds of production workers. At the end of 2016, I started the process of separating each unit of operations in order to make the whole organization work seamlessly as one large corporate entity. Yet the process was long and arduous, and as a result, Lifespan's employee turnover rate rapidly increased. Many employees didn't adjust well to the changes, and before I even realized what was happening, the culture shifted negatively in-house. Originally, I wanted to ensure that all our employees – hundreds of them in 2017 – adapted a cost-conscious attitude while driving efficiency.

However, I began to notice that if I were to focus on one unit's goals, another unit's goals would suffer. Inconsistent outcomes were prominent in the organization as a whole. It was a catch-22, and I was drowning with my responsibilities and those of my employees. As the CEO and a leader, I came to recognize that I had to allow managers to come up with their own solutions for getting the job done. They would have to take responsibility for their actions to ensure the performance of their teams while I continued to communicate the vision and work with the team to creating that winning strategy which would allow us to accomplish our goals as a company.

My training process transitioned immensely and immediately when I decided to make the switch in 2019. I told myself I would no longer micromanage any of my employees. Waiting for others to get the job done was never my strong suit, so letting go of the idea of micromanaging was difficult yet necessary as a leader of a large organization. I've never liked wasting time, as I find time to be a valuable resource. Instead of training someone, I had always figured I would do the job myself, especially if the training was taking too much time away from other necessary tasks. While I slowly decided to step out of my comfort zone, I allowed the General Manager as well as each individual unit manager to take the reins. I wanted every unit of Lifespan to succeed by working together to meet deadlines efficiently and effectively without me having to constantly poke my head into my employees' offices to see how they were doing and whether or not they were on track.

When initially interviewing candidates for roles at Lifespan, I always tended to look at their academic qualifications. But I realized that, just because a candidate went to a prestigious university or had a former job at one of the major corporations, it didn't mean they had the required critical thinking skills or emotional intelligence to grow beyond their norm. In order to cultivate the right team, it took years of trial and error, with lots of money going down the drain as a result of training the wrong employees, who sometimes left their positions after only a short period working with the company. Humans are all designed differently; I had to learn this the hard way and it drove me to strategize and implement new systems.

The core values of Lifespan include happiness and inclusivity. My aim was to create a family-oriented environment. Even though Jamaica itself has its own culture, every individual also comes with their own home culture. We each form our identities from how we grow up, what type of guardians/parents we have, where we go to school, the friends we keep, and much more. Through the training process, I learned to embrace everyone's personality and culture, and I looked for the strengths that they could bring to Lifespan, too. Sometimes, I still found that employees would purposefully be harmful and want to cause harm, which was a difficult notion for me, since I have always, deep down, believed that people are inherently good-hearted and good-natured.

Inconsistencies, I learned, can cost a business dearly, just as much as not having the right team in place can do. Implementing systems were necessary to put an extra layer of protection within the business. I yearned for Lifespan to achieve business continuity, efficiency, accountability, and transparency. Leading my team was critical yet challenging, but I told myself over and over again that I was capable of greatness. I was driven to become not only an entrepreneur, but a high-level leader of a company that I founded.

*

One of the first tasks I knew I needed to hand off was bookkeeping. Throughout the first five to seven years of Lifespan, I did all the bookkeeping, yet it was becoming extremely cumbersome to keep up with this aspect of the business myself, along with my other responsibilities as CEO. I would find myself getting ready for bed at midnight some days, only to realize that I still needed to catch up on bookkeeping from the day before. There were so many evenings where I only got only two hours of sleep, and I was barely spending time with Beth and Milan.

Devon noticed I was drowning in this work as well and offered support.

"So, there's this young man, Alec, who's in his last year at the University of the West Indies," Devon told me one evening while we were laying awake in bed. It was midnight, and he held me while I told him my dilemma. In those days, I could be extremely vulnerable with Devon and receive the support I needed. Though I was normally able to hold everything together in my life, I felt I was breaking apart with the lack of sleep and lack of help with Lifespan.

"I knew this kid's mom when I was growing up," Devon explained. "I hear he's absolutely brilliant and he's majoring in accounting. Why don't we give him a shot? Let's see if he can help us out. That way you could train him, and bookkeeping would be off your plate."

I nodded slowly.

"You're brilliant, Devon!" I kissed him passionately. "Thank you, yes, let's give it a go."

A week later, Devon happened to see Alec walking along the riverside on his way to crab bush. Devon was driving and pulled over to the side of the road. Alec didn't notice him until he called out to him.

"Hey Alec!" Devon exclaimed. "How are you?"

Alec looked confused and a bit bewildered at first, not recognizing Devon. Alec frequently saw Devon in the neighbourhood, but he had never spoken to him before.

"Hi man, can I help you? How do you know my name?" Alec asked curiously. His dark eyes sparkled in the sunlight against his deep melanin skin. He wore khaki shorts and a striped polo shirt, his feet bare, holding a machete in one hand and a burlap bag in the other, a common sight during crab season in Jamaica.

"Oh!" Devon belted out a laugh. "I knew your mother growing up. You're graduating from UWI soon, right?"

"Yes, I'm going to be looking for an accounting job soon," Alec said.

"Well, you're in luck, my friend," Devon exclaimed. "My wife and I own the company Lifespan. We bottle naturally alkaline spring water at our factory, and we've been expanding our market reach. We're actually looking for help in our accounting department. Are you interested in coming to work for us?"

Again, Alec looked stunned.

"I guess, yes, that sounds like a great opportunity, thank you for thinking of me."

"Fantastic! Go to the Lifespan office in Spring Garden today or tomorrow, and ask for my wife, Nayana. She'll start training you."

They shook hands, and the following day, Alec came to my office. After talking with him briefly, I noted he had very little experience, and he still had to complete certain classes before he was eligible to receive his accounting degree.

"I would love to work here," Alec said enthusiastically, looking around my office and then the factory as I gave him a tour. "This looks like such a great environment, and I really want to learn more about the work you're doing here at Lifespan."

He sweet-talked his way into a job at the factory, where he worked in the production department for a year while finishing his accounting degree. After he had proven himself, I moved him into the office as a bookkeeper. I started to give him more and more work, as he was a fast learner. When he finally received his degree, he was promoted to accountant. I was so relieved to have found someone who could take over responsibilities. Though he developed at his own pace, he would always figure out his own way of carrying out each task efficiently, even without me having to explain the task to him verbatim. This was rare in my experience as CEO, and I guided him closely as a cat held onto her string. Devon was extremely pleased as well, knowing that his contribution to the company made my life less hectic, and that we were now able to spend more time together, going on spontaneous lunch dates as we used to do years prior.

After three years, I promoted Alec to Financial Controller of Lifespan. We were all thrilled. I felt excited that I could trust an employee; I trusted him so much in fact, that Lifespan subsidized Alec furthering his education, with the intent of grooming him to become General Manager. I finally felt comfortable letting go of any micromanaging I had once done regarding the company's finances, even though we were still working on finagling together a proper system within the whole organization.

Suddenly, red flags started to appear, which were concerning, yet enlightening. Alec used to be jovial with staff in the administration team and was even invited to their personal events outside of work on a regular basis. But rumors began to circulate that Alec was no longer being kind to anyone on the team, which concerned me. Yet I knew these were just rumors, so I didn't give much thought to them at the time. I brushed off anything negative anyone had to say about Alec, partially because he was my mentee, and partially because Lifespan had invested so much time, energy, and resources into his professional development.

Soon, I was proven wrong. He began having private meetings in his office with employees from various departments, none of which had anything to do with accounting. Whenever I would pass by his office, the door was closed. These meetings were consuming his time, and he began to fall short on his deliverables, which was extremely concerning, since he had always put his work as first priority. Now, deadlines were a thing of the past for Alec.

Finally, I had a meeting with him in my own office.

"Alec, help me understand what's happening," I tried to reason with him. "These spreadsheets aren't adding up, and I've had others complain to me about your behavior recently. I'm ready to bring in HR, but I wanted to talk to you first since we have a good relationship. What is really going on?"

His eyes immediately darted away from me as he stared at the white, tiled floor in my office.

"I have no idea what you mean," he said casually. "I believe I've been meeting my deadlines since the day I started working here."

"You have, until recently," I replied, concerned. I searched his face for any ounce of truth but couldn't find it. I knew then that this was going to be a losing battle.

"Alright, just have these reports on my desk by Tuesday; it's important, as I have a board report to complete and submit before our next board meeting in two weeks," I said, dismissing him from my office. I knew his behavior was a major red flag, yet I didn't have specific proof of what he was actually up to in his office until months later.

Unfortunately, my suspicions were proven correct after I discreetly conducted an investigation. Alec had mishandled the company's funds and had conspired with our insurance agent, a friend of his, to take out life insurance on several employees in the admin department. This was at the company's expense, and benefited the agent's commission. Lifespan spent over $4 million paying for insurance coverage.

When this news hit my desk, I sank into my chair and put my head in my hands. I felt so many emotions rise up inside of myself – anger, frustration, sadness, disappointment, confusion, and much more. Plus, I had so many unanswered questions:

Was I really that terrible of a manager that I couldn't tell when an employee was trying to rob my own company?

How can I trust anyone else I hire?

What if I'm just a bad manager and a bad leader?

Am I really capable of handling these setbacks as a CEO of a major company?

After alerting the insurance company to the discrepancies I discovered, they uncovered a ring of irregularities within their firm, which triggered a massive investigation. Our insurance agent was arrested, and the matter continued in criminal court. I continued with my internal investigation within Lifespan, too, because I needed to find out how long the funds were misappropriated for, and I also felt the need to know exactly how this occurred so the leadership team could prevent fraud from happening again within my company.

After gathering all the intelligence and weighing my options, I eventually decided it wasn't worth my time to legally pursue actions against Alec. I reasoned that, since the insurance company reimbursed us, he was a young man, and he would hopefully learn his lesson and change for the better. Again, time and energy were huge factors in this decision. Others in my life, including Devon and several people on our leadership team, wanted to pursue legal action. But I kept asking myself if the amount of time and energy I would spend on this matter was really worth it. I needed to decide whether or not it was more important to take Alec down in court, or if I should spend my time improving systems within Lifespan so this wouldn't happen again.

This experience taught me a myriad of lessons, all of which led to structural and training improvements within the organization. I knew I needed to begin employing experienced and qualified people who had proven themselves in other places of work in terms of investing within themselves. To this day, the hardest lesson I learned was that I couldn't help every single person who came my way. The idea of giving up on anyone bothered me immensely, as I have always believed that people want to do better and give to this world to the best of their ability. However, some people, like Alec, don't have the patience, drive, and determination to do better, which is still difficult for me to understand. Like many millennials, Alec wanted overnight success which was not possible. Gratitude has always played such an important role in my life, but people, including many employees, don't necessarily believe in gratitude or believe in bettering themselves.

Chapter 25

Becoming Lifespan

The same family members, business associates, friends, and acquaintances who put forth their many doubts about Lifespan in 2006 turned a corner when the company grew larger and larger. Comments such as, "This is a dumb idea" were forgotten and replaced with, "Can I come to the next Lifespan event? I just told my co-worker that you're my niece, and I'm so proud of what you have accomplished!"

Gratitude came into play here once again, as I beamed when I received flattering comments like these. But I didn't have too much time to get caught up in these kind comments; I continued to be my usual courteous self, always accepting and acknowledging when someone else was being kind towards me and my accomplishments as a business leader and innovator.

I continued to attend media appearances, photoshoots galore, and more to expand Lifespan's presence, yet Devon didn't think these were as important as I did. When Lifespan began, I considered Devon and I to be equal partners in building the brand, and he did as well.

Yet our views slowly began to drift in different directions after a period of many years. Though I had forgiven Devon, the initial betrayal that I experienced from his actions still crept into our marriage and resulted in occasional screaming matches which became fewer and fewer as the years went by. As the business progressed, Devon's title remained as CPO of Lifespan for many years. He was not interested in being a part of the day-to-day operations, which left the majority of decision-making power in my hands as CEO. I took charge willingly because I continued to believe in the brand of Lifespan. I was forced to be decisive at the drop of a hat without any complaints. Being present, aware, and dedicated were important traits I needed to have in leading the agenda of the company.

I continued to express gratitude for the numerous opportunities that presented themselves, despite the effects that the business had on my personal life. I constantly analyzed the market, consumer needs, the competitive landscape, the economical and political impacts, as well as the threats and opportunities that presented themselves. Once I had more systems in place where I no longer needed to micromanage my departments, I was able to spend more time with my family, which I cherished and never took for granted. Rather than staying up for hours all night long, I was able to be home with my children and Devon and prepare dinner for them around 7 p.m. each night. I ensured my home was stocked with the requisite supplies while my helpers in the home were well-attuned to my family's expectations. Beth and I would watch movies, read books, and spend quality time together until she fell asleep. Milan would sometimes ask for help with his homework, and I immediately obliged, knowing that this was another opportunity to help my son, and also to connect with him on a deeper level. When Milan started high school, he would call me via FaceTime while he completed his assignments, and I felt lucky to have helped him through this incredible virtual option. He wanted me to be present more, and so I obliged, because he asked, and because I would do anything for my children. As he grew older, the FaceTime calls lessened, yet we still used this technology when he had a specific question about a homework assignment.

After our children went to bed, Devon and I occasionally watched TV together, or just talked about life and just enjoyed each other's company. More often than not, the subject of Lifespan came up, since the business was ingrained in our personal lives.

*

As the years trickled on, Lifespan became more well-known. We would pay for billboard advertisements, TV ads, magazine ads, and much more. I was making a media appearance at least twice a month by 2014, which was when the company was selected as a Bold One of Manufacturing by the National Continental Baking Company. Word was also getting out through social media and Lifespan's raving fans – those consumers who had a testimony of Lifespan to share publicly. The greatest media exposure we received was my participation in the NCB Capital Quest reality TV Show, which had some similarities to the American reality TV series, *Shark Tank*. We had the opportunity to pitch the business to investors for a chance to win a $50 million investment. NCB Capital Quest portrayed a group of businesses competing for this investment, and each business needed to go through several developmental stages until every individual was prepared. I went to the set almost every day for weeks for filming.

At filming of the final episode, Devon and I had planned to do our Lifespan presentation together in front of the investors. We had practiced and prepared for days on end. This was an enormous opportunity for Lifespan's growth, as well as our own financial growth. We had both memorized different aspects of the brand from spreadsheets, including projected budgets, employee numbers, distribution factors, production, and much more.

But the morning of the interview, Devon changed his tune.

"I don't think we're going to win, Sandy," he said at 6:30 a.m. "Let's not go."

We were scheduled to be in Kingston together at 10:00 a.m., and it would take about an hour and a half to get there.

I froze. My makeup brush stood still in my hands. Blush covered our bathroom counter. A minute ago, I felt elated to have this incredible opportunity. I was so grateful that we would be doing this together; we were a true power couple who could go the distance together, both inside of our home and within our business. But this notion dissipated as soon as he said those words aloud.

"Devon," I sighed, turning towards him. He was sitting on our bed, refusing to get dressed now. "Please, we both worked so hard to do this. It'll be a great experience and exposure for the brand, even if you're right and we don't win. Let's get ready and go. Please?"

I was on the verge of tears, begging him. I had no idea what I was going to do. When you're in a state of shock and panic, you aren't necessarily thinking straight.

"Sandy, I'm not going." His voice flattened, and I couldn't hear an ounce of emotion within his words.

"But I'm confused," I said to him. "We've worked on our presentation for the past few weeks. I thought this was something you wanted too?"

He laughed bitterly.

"Absolutely not, this was your idea, and I did this to appease you, but now I'm done. I'm getting ready, and I'm going to work now. Do you remember the company we have? Let's concentrate on what we have rather than what we don't have. Do whatever you want without me."

He jumped out of bed, threw on his clothes, and took off in his Isuzu pickup truck. Within five minutes, he was gone, and I was left with streaming mascara down my cheeks. When Devon and I had these types of arguments, I would occasionally ask my father-in-law for advice, since he knew Devon better than anyone, including myself.

Luckily, Mr. Joe lived a few streets away, and his daily routine included walking to our home in the early mornings for exercise, so when I called him in tears, his response was that he was right outside. He found me in a crumpled mess atop of Elizabeth's bed at 7 a.m. I was still wearing pajamas, and makeup was strewn across my face. All in all, I was a complete disaster.

"Mr.—" I couldn't even get his name out without crying. "He... left... the... film... ing…"

"Shh, I understand, Sandy," he said as he patted my shoulder. Sometimes when you're in distress, the best thing is a listening ear from a loved one.

"Don't listen to Devon, he's being an idiot," Mr. Joe said casually. "Look at me. You've been talking about this filming for weeks now. I see you light up. You're on fire. Lifespan is booming. To hell with what Devon says. You do this yourself."

I wiped my tears away, giving my hands black tattoos from the mascara that covered my eyelashes just a half hour prior.

"Pick yourself back up. Dust yourself off. Get moving," he told me. "You don't have a ton of time. But you have the drive to calm yourself down, so use it wisely."

Before he left, he made sure I was standing and smiling.

"Thank you, Mr. Joe," I said, beaming at him. "Thank you."

I washed off my face and my hands and jumped in the shower, my second one that morning. I needed to feel refreshed and renewed, and I knew a quick shower could do the trick. I listened to Mr. Joe, but I also listened to myself that day. This was a rare and special opportunity for Lifespan, and I wasn't going to let that go just because my husband/business partner decided to stomp all over it a few hours before filming. Additionally, I knew that the exposure that Lifespan would get alone would impact sales positively; plus, I would never quit something in the middle. I had finished all my schooling, all my programmes, and had seen everything to completion. This TV show was no different; I would see this through, despite my emotions surrounding the whole ordeal.

Though Devon was partially right – we didn't win – the show still exposed our brand to Jamaica, and to audiences who had never heard of Lifespan before. Going on the show was also a huge personal growth opportunity for me as well; it opened my eyes, and more doors, to media appearances, ones in which I used to watch as a kid, and now I was being invited to be interviewed about the company I co-founded. In 2015, we contracted a mentor/coach for Lifespan and formalized the board as well, giving way to proper corporate governance, increased sales, increased marketing, increased distribution, and increased production, all of which gave Lifespan more credibility.

Chapter 26

A Celebration of Wins

In 2017, I finally felt I could breathe. Our entire team, consisting of more than 200 employees and contractors, seemed happy and thriving at Lifespan. The retention rate at the company increased, and bonuses were handed out like hotcakes that year. I felt motivated and grateful that the leadership team had started the successful implementation of systems we had been working on for years. We had achieved a great deal that year. It was time to celebrate our wins with a party.

Over 250 people were in attendance, including the Lifespan team, vendors, suppliers, customers, friends, and family. It was a festive night with our celebrity ambassador serving as our master of ceremonies in partnership with a male counterpart, a very dynamic duo that evening. They stood at the glass podium in front of a crystal-white glistening backdrop, engaging the crowd who erupted in laughter. A songstress belted out her smooth reggae lyrics while the audience rocked to the beat. Our then distributor sponsored the bar and champagne flowed throughout the night. The food was a delectable array of Jamaican dishes from a local caterer while desserts were from the famous Chocolate Dreams in Kingston. The evening was a success with all the guests looking elegant in their black and white attire. There were still some naysayers in the family who came just to glare at me; their dagger-like stares were caught on camera when I went up to the podium for my CEO speech. Although I wore a brave face, as I always do when appearing in public, I felt incredibly uncomfortable and somewhat sad. Time and time again, these relatives pushed their own uncertainties about themselves and their futures onto others, including me, and they were angry at my success. They completely alienated themselves, yet expected to be invited to parties, like this one, even though they pouted and crossed their arms around their chests all night long.

But I couldn't concentrate on those death-like stares all night.

A handful of disgruntled people shouldn't discount the work I've put into the business, and so I decided to focus on my guests, my team, other relatives, and friends who were happy for me and happy for Lifespan's achievements.

I reminded myself that I couldn't please everyone, and as a business leader, I couldn't expect to please every single person in my life; some folks just can't be happy for others when they find success. I recognized that no matter what I did, said, or how successful or unsuccessful I was, it was never enough. They viewed the business as its own separate entity, completely separate from me, its CEO. It was either too painful or too detrimental to them to simply accept that I played a huge role in developing Lifespan to what it was becoming – an extremely successful product in the Jamaican marketplace, and soon, in the world.

Throughout my tenure as CEO, I was taunted and told that all I wanted was fame for myself. My marriage grew more and more strained every single day. Emotional and verbal insults were thrown my way daily. Though I continued to be brave and fearless, sometimes, hearing and taking in this type of taunting was just too much. I remembered the last time I had a panic attack, right before the Elders came into my life, and how I looked towards God for help during these moments of crises. I would sit in my hammock in the front of my yard, or I would swim in our outdoor pool, letting the sunshine radiate across my face. Feeling the warm air on my skin always helped me avoid a nervous breakdown, even though I felt myself come to that point many times over, especially in 2018 and in 2019. It was difficult to maintain all my business and personal relationships, as many, including my marriage, were intertwined.

Towards the beginning of 2018, I instructed my mentee to carry out my responsibilities while I mostly worked away from the office. I knew that by not being at Lifespan's offices physically, the bullies would have less opportunities to berate me. The constant, overwhelming pressure from certain relatives became unbearable. When you've experienced the dynamics of the different relations over the many years, you expect, and even anticipate, that relationships will change; that some will blossom, and some will fall apart. It got to a point where I found the sacred space of my marriage being breached by others due to their attempts to insert themselves into my personal and professional life. I felt that if I confided certain information to those closest to me, other relatives would immediately become aware of what I had said in confidence; then I would be the beneficiary of their misperceptions and nasty remarks, sometimes being chastised to total strangers. I became sad, infuriated, and confused as to why my personal and professional actions became the interest of others.

There were several instances where I had to talk myself out of throwing everything away that I had built, which is a common occurrence in entrepreneurship when the road becomes tougher than you may ever expect. I typed up a resignation letter once but never sent it. I almost left my family one evening after packing a duffel bag. Instead, I unpacked the bag mere minutes later. The insides of the bag were a jumbled mess, and I cried as I threw everything out onto the floor of my home office, not bothering to look and see what was there until days later.

My marriage became more than just the two of us. There were now multiple people involved. It was like a clown car, like it was everyone else's marriage but mine. The business became the primary focus of everyone. It was like there was no clear line of separation when it came to my marriage and the business. I felt that I was no longer a priority to my husband at one point; it was more important to confide or receive advice from other relatives than me. I was often misjudged and condemned for my actions which were in the best interest of the business and its shareholders.

Soon, though, I stood my ground once again, stronger than I ever thought I could be. I knew I needed to find a healthy way to deal with this additional pressure, and so, once again, I focused on what I could control – my own choices and my own life. I began to ignore any slander thrown my way, knowing that the words were wrong, and my inner critic didn't have to acknowledge them. Over the years, I have continued to grow and learn so much, especially when it comes to pleasing others. Releasing myself from binding, displeasing situations has been extremely refreshing, as I know that I alone have control over my life, my thoughts, and my actions. I forgave those who misjudged and slandered me and prayed for clarity and blessings to them.

I continued to be grateful, however, for my marriage and my relatives, because this situation, once again, propelled me forward. I knew that I could muster the courage and tenacity to move into my future with the utmost strength and understanding that I was in charge of how I felt. As Eleanor Roosevelt once said, "No one can make you feel inferior, except yourself."

After a short period of time, I realized that I had made a mistake by allowing my mentee to take charge of my tasks. Managing Lifespan at a distance, at this level, wasn't an option, and unfortunately, many mishaps took place as a result. Though I delegated responsibilities to those I thought I could trust, once again, I was betrayed by several employees. They intentionally manipulated the situation by milking money from Lifespan using vendors whom they were close with. Lifespan ended up having many excess payments where overspending took place unnecessarily. I was heartbroken at this betrayal once again, yet I continued to learn from my mistakes and experiences. This also helped me understand where my own responsibilities should be within the organization, especially while dealing with personal turmoil.

Though I had decided years ago to hire qualified people, I still needed to work on picking employees whom I could develop a trusting relationship with. We restructured the hiring process once again, using a third-party source this time around, which helped immensely. Although it took many months to develop a proper structure and systems between teams, having this collaborative environment was extraordinarily helpful as I fully adapted into my role of leading the organization once again.

As I continued to learn and grow as CEO, I sometimes lost direct sight into specific areas of the company, which negatively impacted sales. Lifespan saw several long-standing relationships crumble due to new hires, who were not quite understanding of the culture of the company. While I knew that these individuals had their own talents and their own home cultures, I still needed to not only find qualified employees, but also ones who were adaptable. Yet the damage was already done. Every change requires a risk analysis and an action plan in order to mitigate the possible risk factors.

As the demand for our bottled water grew, Lifespan progressed tenfold. We were able to complete our capacity build out after receiving several capital injections over several years. Lifespan employed more than 160 people, half being production workers. After a firm evaluation, the leadership team decided to hire an outsourcing company to supply production workers rather than having direct employees, causing a massive layoff at Lifespan.

Since Lifespan was created, we had distributed 50% of what we produced directly, and the other half was distributed by a major distributor. This hybrid model was working well, since the intention was to build out sales, merchandising, and logistics. Ultimately, my goal was to have the company become 100% self-sufficient. Yet the pandemic proved this notion to be faulty, and we encountered additional challenges.

We were also transitioning distributors once again, yet the new one proved to be less effective than the previous. They were extremely inconsistent during our high season, summer, and I met with them in the middle of 2020.

"Listen, I'm ready to terminate our agreement," I told the distribution manager over a video call.

"Please, Nayana, this is a hard year for all of us," he said as he winced in his black chair, his left leg shaking the ground beneath him. "I'm not begging you, but this is as close as I'll get. Would you consider giving us some type of probation period? We'll try to do better, I promise."

I was sick of empty promises from those I thought I could trust. So many relationships in my life had come to a nasty end based on betrayal and distrust. I was no stranger to negotiating deals, but after fifteen years, I was surely not going to be an easy target.

"Alright, listen, I'll give you a ninety-day probation period," I sighed. "I know your proposed targets are below our projections, but let's try it. That way, we'll know how your targets are doing, and we'll make a determination at that time of our work together."

I clicked "Leave Meeting" on my computer, unsure of my decision, but simultaneously hoping this would work. I still believed in the goodness of people and their hearts, despite all the tumultuous relationships in my own life.

Ninety days went by quickly. Because of the distributor's reduced numbers, our direct distribution arm would have to make up the difference. My team ultimately pulled this off, and this experience strengthened our own direct distribution, sales team, and merchandising, all of which was fantastic for in-house camaraderie and career development.

Though Lifespan managed to survive, as so many businesses did not, I consider Lifespan to be starting anew once again after dealing with an extraordinary year.

*

Battles continue to be won and lost as an entrepreneur. For instance, we contracted a major distributor many years ago, and though everything was going smoothly at first, they suddenly stopped paying us while stockpiling our products in their warehouse and stopped fulfilling orders to the trades with the intention to put us in a position to sell the company at a minimum. Every time I encounter a new lesson, I take it in and acknowledge how far I've come – and how far Lifespan has come.

Major companies have wanted to purchase Lifespan over the years. While I felt flattered that these corporations saw the value in our brand, the offers we received were extremely low, even bordering on offensive. Devon and I built this business from the ground up through sacrifice, sweat, and tears. Together, we have weathered many storms, and continue to navigate through life together. Lifespan isn't merely a business, though. It is a movement. It is an iconic brand. It is my legacy that I'm leaving behind for my children, my community, and numerous others.

My experiences are what have molded me into becoming who I am today. I have no regrets; despite the many mistakes I have made as CEO. The lessons we learn along the way are what prepares us for the next chapter on our journey. It would be misleading to say that there's a clear path void of obstacles; this is simply a fallacy, as there are always obstructions in your way. Roadblocks can seem extremely discouraging, but like I always tell Milan, "Pick yourself up, brush yourself off, and continue on… but feel free to cry and let out the frustration if you need to. Spend five minutes feeling your feelings, because time is of the essence. Time is your most precious resource, and time wasted cannot be regained."

The way in which we manage our experiences and the lessons we learn is not only telling of our leadership qualities, but it ultimately makes us who we are. How we respond and grow is what makes the difference. We can choose to *control* a situation or be *controlled by* the situation.

Four main takeaways I've learned throughout my tenure as CEO include:

1. My thoughts are what manifest my reality.
2. My ability to compartmentalize has led me to successfully carry out my duties.
3. Expressing gratitude every step of the way has allowed me to achieve happiness through it all.
4. Always do what must be done in the short term to sustain the business for the long term.

While I often put on a fearless, brave face, people who didn't know me well would say, "How are you coping? It seems like you have no stress at all. This business seems so easy, maybe I should start a bottled water company!"

I would smile and laugh, ensuring them that this was not simply a "walk in the park," but that there are ways in which I manage stress. Drinking enough water, eating the right foods, having close-knit relationships, positive self-talk, compartmentalizing my different roles and responsibilities and more are only a few of the ways I've been able to handle stressful situations in my life.

Life is a continuous roller coaster of ups and downs. When I look back at where I was, both personally and professionally, to where I am now, I feel proud of myself, and proud of the decisions I've made through the years. My greatest satisfaction to this date is seeing how Lifespan has positively impacted millions of lives. This is my greatest pride and joy, as well as my greatest motivation.

Most of all, I'm always grateful for the many accomplishments I have achieved by myself and with others. Yet there is still much more for me to do in setting examples for future generations, specifically up and coming female leaders who have innovative ideas for the marketplace. You, too, can do your part in preserving, maintaining, and building a healthier world.

Nayana Williams is an award-winning CEO, philanthropist, and passionate leader. In 2005, she co-founded Lifespan Company Limited, one of Jamaica's leading bottled water manufacturing companies. The celebrated story and success of today was not without challenges and lessons, along the way. Nayana built Lifespan from the ground up, catapulting it into becoming a market leader in a male-dominated industry. Lifespan has gone on to become an iconic brand, the recipient of multiple international awards and several local awards and nominations.

Nayana lives with her husband, two children and five dogs. Her many roles include being a wife, mother, daughter, sister, and mentor to emerging entrepreneurs. She holds multiple degrees in business, and a law degree. Nayana enjoys reading, writing, swimming and cooking among other pastimes when she is not busy building business and giving back to the community. An avid adventurer, an amateur artist, and an analyst, she considers each day as an opportunity to be a ceaseless student of philosophy, a lover of life, and a source of hope and kindness.